STRATIFICATION *and* DIFFERENTIATION

Janis Griffiths and Tanya Hope

Series Editor: Paul Selfe

Hodder & Stoughton
A MEMBER OF THE HODDER HEADLINE GROUP

DEDICATION

We would like to dedicate this book to our families and friends, for all their support while writing was in progress.

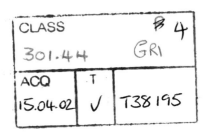

Orders: please contact Bookpoint Ltd, 39 Milton Park, Abingdon, Oxon OX14 4TD. Telephone: (44) 01235 400414, Fax: (44) 01235 400454. Lines are open from 9.00–6.00, Monday to Saturday, with a 24 hour message answering service. Email address: orders@bookpoint.co.uk

A catalogue record for this title is available from The British Library

ISBN 0 340 73760 3

First published 2000
Impression number 10 9 8 7 6 5 4 3 2 1
Year   2005 2004 2003 2002 2001 2000

Cover painting by L.S. Lowry – *The Pond*, c.o. The Tate Gallery

Typeset by Transet Limited, Coventry, England.
Printed in Great Britain for Hodder & Stoughton Educational, a division of Hodder Headline plc, 338 Euston Road, London NW1 3BH by Redwood Books, Trowbridge, Wilts.

CONTENTS

ACKNOWLEDGEMENTS

The publishers would like to thank Davies/Hulton Getty picture collection for permission to reproduce the photograph on page 38, and Richard Hamilton-Smith/Corbis for the photograph on page 104.

1

INTRODUCTION

HOW TO USE THE BOOK

EACH CHAPTER IN this book examines one or more of the central debates relating to the sociology of families. The text is devised for readers with little or no background knowledge in the subject, and there are Study Points and Activities throughout to encourage a consideration of the issues raised. Student readers are advised to make use of these and answer them either on paper or in group discussion, a particularly fruitful way of learning; they will assist them to develop the skills of interpretation, analysis and evaluation. There are many ways of preparing for an exam, but a thorough understanding of the material is obviously crucial.

Each chapter is structured to give a clear understanding of the authors, concepts and issues that you need to know about. To assist understanding and facilitate later revision, it is often helpful to make concise notes.

MAKING NOTES FROM THE BOOK

Linear notes
- Bold headings establish key points: names, theories and concepts.
- Subheadings indicate details of relevant issues.
- A few numbered points list related arguments.

Diagram or pattern notes
- Use a large blank sheet of paper and write a key idea in the centre.
- Make links between this and related issues.
- Show also the connections between sub issues which share features in common.

Both systems have their advantages and disadvantages, and may take some time to perfect. Linear notes can be little more than a copy of what is already in the book and patterned notes can be confusing. But if you practise the skill, they can reduce material efficiently and concisely becoming invaluable for revision. Diagrammatic notes may be very useful for those with a strong visual memory and provide a clear overview of a whole issue, showing patterns of interconnection. The introduction of helpful drawings or a touch of humour into the format is often a good way to facilitate the recall of names, research studies and complex concepts.

Activity

Make a diagram to show the two ways of making notes with their possible advantages and disadvantages

SKILLS ADVICE

Students must develop and display certain skills for their examination and recognise which ones are being tested in a question. The clues are frequently in key words in the opening part. The skill domains are:

1   **Knowledge and understanding:** the ability to discuss the views of the main theorists; their similarities and differences; the strengths and weaknesses of evidence. To gain marks students must display this when asked to *explain, examine, suggest a method, outline reasons.*
2   **Interpretation, application and analysis:** the use of evidence in a logical, relevant way, either to show how it supports arguments or refutes them. Students must show this ability when asked *identify, use items A/B/C, draw conclusions from a table.*
3   **Evaluation:** the skill of assessing evidence in a balanced way so that logical conclusions follow. Students can recognise this skill when asked to *assess, critically examine, comment on levels of reliability, compare and contrast,* or if asked *to what extent.*

Activity

Draw an evaluation table, as below, using the whole of an A4 page. Examine studies as you proceed in your work and fill in the relevant details. Keep it for revision purposes.

Sociologist		
Title of the study	Strengths	Weaknesses
Verdict		
Judgement/justification		

REVISION ADVICE

- Keep clear notes at all times in a file or on disk (with back up copy).
- Be familiar with exam papers and their demands.
- Become familiar with key authors, their theories, their research and sociological concepts.

COLLECTIVE CONSCIENCE

Key idea

A term used by **Durkheim** meaning:

- The existence of a social and moral order exterior to individuals and acting upon them as an independent force.
- The shared sentiments, beliefs and values of individuals which make up the **collective conscience.**
- In **traditional societies** it forms the basis of social order.
- As societies modernise the collective conscience weakens: **mechanical solidarity** is replaced by **organic solidarity**.

Key theorist: Emile Durkheim

Syllabus area: Functionalism

EXAMINATION ADVICE

To develop an effective method of writing, answers should be:

- **Sociological:** use the language and research findings of sociologists; do not use anecdotal opinion gathered from people not involved in sociology to support arguments.
- **Adequate in length:** enough is written to obtain the marks available.
- **Interconnected** with other parts of the syllabus (such as stratification, gender, ethnicity).
- **Logical:** the answer follows from the relevant evidence.
- **Balanced:** arguments and counter arguments are weighed; references are suitable.
- **Accurate:** reliable data is obtained from many sources.

The three skill areas on p 2 should be demonstrated, so that the question is answered effectively.

In displaying knowledge, the student is not necessarily also demonstrating interpretation.

- This must be specified with phrases like 'Therefore, this study leads to the view that...'
- Sections of answers should hang together, one leading to the next. This shows how the question is being answered by a process of analysis based on the evidence.
- Reach a conclusion based on the evidence used and the interpretations made.

The skill of evaluation is often regarded (not necessarily accurately) as the most problematic. Evaluation means being judge and jury; the strengths and weaknesses of evidence is assessed and an overall judgement about its value is made. To evaluate an argument or theory, consider whether it usefully opens up debate; explains the events studied; does it have major weaknesses?

Activity

Look through some past examination papers and pick out the evaluation questions. Underline the evaluation words and work out which skills are required.

COURSEWORK ADVICE

Coursework provides an opportunity to carry out a study using primary and/or secondary data to investigate an issue of sociological interest, and must address theoretical issues. The suggestions included at the end of each chapter may be adapted or used to generate further ideas. Final decision must be agreed with a teacher or tutor.

MAKING A PLAN

Before starting a piece of coursework, you should make a plan:

1 Read and make notes from articles describing research projects in journals.
2 Have a clear aim in mind; choose an issue that interests you and is within your ability.
3 Decide more precisely what you want to know; establish a simple hypothesis to test.

4 Select a range of possible methods; consider both quantitative and qualitative.
5 Decide on a range of possible sources of information.
6 List the people to whom you can seek help, perhaps including a statistician.

WRITING THE PROJECT

1 Seek frequent advice from a teacher or tutor.
2 Check the weighting for different objectives in the marking scheme.
3 Keep clear notes throughout, including new ideas and any problems that arise.
4 Limit its length (maximum 5,000 words).
5 Label and index the study in the following way:

   a **Rationale:** a reason for choosing the subject; preliminary observations on the chosen area
   b **Context:** an outline of the theoretical and empirical context of the study
   c **Methodology:** a statement of the methodology used and reasons for selecting it
   d **Content:** presentation of the evidence and/or argument including results
   e **Evaluation:** the outcomes are weighed and strengths and weaknesses noted.
   f **Sources:** all the sources of information are listed.

OR

   a **Title**
   b **Contents**
   c **Abstract:** a brief summary of the aims, methods, findings and evaluation.
   d **Rationale**
   e **The Study**
   f **Research Diary**
   g **Bibliography**
   h **Appendix:** to include proposal for the study, single examples of a questionnaire or other data-gathering instrument and transcripts of interviews.
   i **Annex:** to include raw data gathered.

Paul Selfe
Series editor

2

PERSPECTIVES ON CLASS AND STATUS

Introduction

THIS CHAPTER IS concerned with offering the student an overview of the various ways in which the subject of social class has been approached by sociologists:

- The changing definitions
- The debates arising from the work of Marx (1818–83) and Weber (1864–1920)
- Contemporary theories

Table 1: *Theories, concepts and issues in this chapter*		
WRITERS	CONCEPTS AND CONCERNS	KEY ISSUES
Objective and subjective class	Defining and operationalising class	Can class be measured?
The Registrar General's Index of Social Class, 1911 The National Statistics Socio-Economic Classification, 2001	Classifying a population and using occupation as the basis of classification	Do these classification groups actually form recognisable social groups?
Marxism	Development of classes Growth of proletariat	What is the relationship between the growth of classes and the economy?

	Relationship between proletariat and bourgeoisie	What is the relationship between the growth of classes and the economy?
Weberianism	The link between class and status, party and power The development of plural classes	How useful is this type of theorising when applied to our society?
Parsons (1951) Davis and Moore (1945)	Functionalism	Class-based stratification enables society to function effectively.
Wright (1997) Parkin (1979)	Neo-Marxism	The changing relationships between the classes.
Goldthorpe (1987) Halsey (1978)	Neo-Weberian	A model of social inequality through occupational status.
Runciman (1990)	Structuration	A link between structure and action in class analysis?
Hutton (1995)	New Left	Social inequality enhances class divisions.
Saunders (1995)	New Right	An equal chance to become unequal?

Study point

Decide on all of the things, which you consider give an indication of a person's class. These signals are known as **indices of class**. Your list of indicators of class will probably include such pointers as the kind of education that people have, the way that they speak and their choice of hobbies. How reliable are they?

CLASS AND SOCIAL DEFINITIONS

The term 'social class' has two broad meanings. In daily use, the term refers to a form of social categorisation. In our culture, we are fully aware that some people can claim a higher position in society than we do; we may also consider ourselves to be superior to others. Terms such as 'snob', 'posh' or 'common' give clues to common sense understandings of these differences. Commonplace analyses of class suggest that there are three groups within society: 'working', 'middle' and 'upper' class. We will probably all allocate ourselves to one of these social groups with very little difficulty. This is known as subjective class, but it is very difficult to measure accurately. Practically, while we all have clear personal perceptions of what these terms mean, there is no guarantee that we all share the same understandings.

In sociological terms, class can be seen in two ways:

- It is a term used to describe certain **cultural and lifestyle** habits of groups of people.
- It can be seen as an **economic status** which reflects occupation, education, wealth and prestige.

It can be difficult to separate the two analyses, because obviously wealth and educational status will also dictate cultural and lifestyle choices. This makes the problem of identifying and analysing social class in any practical sense extremely difficult.

Activity

Ask a variety of people their occupation and their sense where they belong in the class structure. It is a safe guess to suggest that most will define themselves as belonging to either the 'upper', 'middle' or 'working' class. Ask your respondents how they recognise their class position and you will have some very interesting qualitative insights into everyday identifiers of social class. Keep notes of this work because you may wish to return to it in further discussion.

OBJECTIVE AND SUBJECTIVE NOTIONS OF CLASS

The classical sociologists, Marx and Weber tended to be concerned with objective accounts of class which relied upon concrete variables which could be measured and noted such as income and occupation. Marx was more successful than Weber in this regard. One of the insights which interpretative sociology has brought to the study of class is the perception that what we feel and understand is of enormous significance to how we behave. Our subjective notions of our class can have an impact on our actions and our morality. **Crewe (1992)**, noted that people's beliefs about their social class were of as much relevance to their voting behaviour, for instance, than any measure of class devised and used by a statistician or sociologist.

- *Objective class* refers to our possessions and our wealth. It can be measured in the data put out by the Office of Population, Censuses and Surveys such as mortality and morbidity lists.

- *Subjective class* refers to our beliefs about our class position and to our norms, morals and values. It can be measured by our attitudes, our beliefs and our political opinions.

GOVERNMENT DEFINITIONS OF SOCIAL CLASS IN MODERN BRITAIN

One of the most common bases for allocating social class is occupation, which is referred to as an objective class measurement. A person's job may reliably be used to indicate a variety of things about them, such as leisure activity, income, education, health and wealth, providing a measurable indicator of class status outside of the individual's own perception.

THE REGISTRAR GENERAL'S INDEX OF SOCIAL CLASS

The Registrar General is a government official. The department run by the Registrar General is the Office of Population Censuses and Surveys and its role is to enumerate the population of Britain in order to aid social policy-making. In 1911, the Registrar General's Office decided upon a system for allocating class to people, which will be used until the year 2001. It is the basis of all systems of class division but is qualitatively very different from the ideas that we have of calling people 'upper class' or 'lower class'. This system attempts to be value free and scientific and allocates people to a class based on their occupation or job. It is known as the **Registrar General's Index of Social Class**. It is also called the RG's Index. This system is a way of describing people for the benefit of planners and marketing. It is used in all government statistics and you must learn it.

Here is the index in simple form:

Table 2			
NUMBER	LETTER		TYPICAL OCCUPATIONS OR JOBS
1	A	Non-manual workers	top management, surgeons, top doctors, university lecturers, chemists
2	B		teachers, executives, journalists
3a	C1	Manual workers	secretaries, sales executives, officials
3b	C2		skilled craftspeople and hairdressers
4	D		semi-skilled people such as bus drivers and machine operators
5	E		unskilled people, labourers and cleaners

- People from classes 1 and 2 are sometimes known as **non-manual workers** because they work using educational skills. These people are also known as **professional** people and in America are called **white-collar workers** because they wear white shirts to work.
- People in classes 3–5 are usually known as **manual workers** because they work with skills using their hands. In America, they are known as **blue-collar workers**.

Criticisms of the Registrar General's Index

This system of measuring class is very widely used, but not very efficient. Among the many criticisms of the index which were made were the following points:

- Women are allocated class based on their nearest male relative. Pensioners and the unemployed are allocated class based on the last job that they did and children gain class from their father's class. This is an important criticism because large numbers of women work, and they are mostly found in lower status jobs such as caring or cleaning.
- Jobs are not always allocated because of skill. Pay and the cleanliness of the job may count too. A checkout worker is in class 3a despite being less skilled than a butcher or a baker.
- People may be underemployed and have a high status education but they are actually employed in jobs that require few skills through choice or bad luck.
- Sometimes jobs are moved class, so postal workers went from class 3 to class 4 in 1961. Clerks have moved down the social scale from a high status occupation to a relatively low status occupation since the advent of office technology and the feminisation of the work.
- Pay scales in the top-job categories of class 1 are quite different. One person may earn only £20,000 while another will earn £200,000 each year.
- Almost the entire population is in class 3a or 3b. This makes the analysis on offer very clumsy as it does not distinguish between groups of people.
- Males engaged in unskilled work in class 5 (dustmen, labourers etc) could earn more money than those in low-status feminised professions such as health ancillary work (speech therapy, physiotherapy etc) which is in class 1.

While the Registrar General's Index of Social Class has always been heavily criticised by sociologists and remains a very blunt tool of analysis, nevertheless significant patterns of social differences become very clear between the various classes. Mortality, educational achievement, birth rates, divorce rates, criminal conviction rates and health patterns are all very different for the social classes represented in the figures, with those at the lower end usually appearing to have a far worse life experience than those in the higher tiers.

THE NATIONAL STATISTICS SOCIO-ECONOMIC CLASSIFICATION – 2001

Changes to the Registrar General's Index of Social Class, which will be used for the new census in 2001, were announced on 1 December 1998. This will replace the index used first in 1911 and will take account of changes in modern society and social structure. The leader of the team who redesigned the class index was Prof. David Rose of Essex University.

The reasons for redesigning were:

1. Manufacturing has declined
2. Under the old system, almost everybody was in class 3
3. The growth in the employment of women
4. The emergence of service sector industry (leisure, food, entertainment, insurance and business)

The basis of the new system is on employment conditions as opposed to just occupation:

1. Job security
2. Promotion opportunity
3. Ability and opportunity to work on own and make own decisions about tasks.

Table 3		
SOCIAL CLASS		TYPICAL EMPLOYMENT
Higher managerial occupations	1.1	Company directors, police Inspectors, bank managers, senior civil servants, military officers
	1.2	Doctor, barrister, solicitor, clergy, librarian, teacher
Lower managerial	2	Nurses and midwives, journalists, actors, prison officers, police and soldiers (below NCO)
Intermediate	3	Clerks, secretaries, driving instructors, computer operator
Small employers	4	Publicans, farmers, Playgroup leader, window cleaner, painter and decorator
Lower supervisory and craft	5	Printers, plumbers, butchers, bus inspectors, TV engineers, train drivers
Semi-routine occupations	6	Shop assistant, traffic warden, cook, bus drivers, hairdressers, postal workers
Routine occupations	7	Waiters, road sweepers, cleaners, couriers, building labourers, refuse collectors
Never worked	8	Long term unemployed and non-workers

Evaluation

1   How is this system different from the old five-category system?
2   Why was it necessary to change the system of classifying people?
3   Do you approve of / agree with this new system? Give sociological reasons for your answer.

INDICES OF CLASS MEMBERSHIP

There is an additional problem with the Registrar General's Index and other indices of social class based upon occupation in that they group together huge populations of people and make assumptions about their behaviour and values on the basis of one variable. Are we really to assume that all the people who fit into either version of the Registrar General's Index Occupational Status Group 1 share a great deal in common because they appear to have superficial similarities of work? This is a very significant point of discussion because it forms part of Marxist analyses of the development of social class. The important question is, do social classes form distinct social groups?

Sociologists would suggest that social groups share cultural norms and patterns of behaviour. By using this definition of a social group, social classes do not form single unified groups, but are better described as **social groupings**. The reason for this suggestion is that:

- Social classes are not officially recognised in any form
- They do not have distinct and clear boundaries
- They do not have a clear membership
- Their significance for many people is qualitative in that behaviour is more likely to be influenced by personal beliefs about class position than any allocation to it by an official or academician.

It is important to remember that there are many different sociological classifications of social class by occupation, which are generally dependent on the theoretical context within which the sociologist is working. The table below provides examples of social-class classifications that have been constructed to determine the amount of people in specific occupational groupings as a reflection of their social status.

Table 4: *Further Sociological Classifications of Social Class Based on Occupation*

NAME OF CLASSIFICATION	SOCIOLOGICAL CONTEXT	REASON FOR DEVELOPMENT
Standard Occupational Classification (1988)	Developed by the Institute for Employment Research	Potential replacement for the RG Index based on more occupational groups without reference to social status.
Essex University Class Scale (Marshall, Newby, Rose and Vogler, 1988)	Neo-Weberian and Neo-Marxist	Provided a classification system for both men women based on occupation.
Surrey Occupational Class Scale (Arber, Dale and Gilbert, 1986)	Feminist	Replaced notion of 'head of household' (usually the man) dictating class with individual class analysis.
Wright Occupational Scale (1997)	Neo-Marxist	Developed to show the exploitative nature of social class.

Golthorpe Occupational Scale (1987)	Neo-Weberian	Combined work situation and marked situation into a unified model of social class.
Runciman Occupational Scale (1990)	Marxist and Weberian	Ownership, marketability and control are united to construct a class-based model of contemporary Britain.
Hutton 30:30:40 Thesis (1995)	New Left	Demonstrates social inequality through a three-way divide in society.

CLASSICAL THEORIES OF CLASS

The two most influential writers on the study of social class were Marx and Weber. Marx was the earlier writer and his theories of social class underlie all of his political and philosophical understandings. He was a revolutionary and was concerned with offering an analysis of contemporary society that explained the exploitation, inequality and poverty that he could see all around him. Weber, however, saw Marxian analysis as simplistic and viewed his own theorising as a corrective to the Marxist view of the development of social class.

MARXIST THEORIES OF CLASS

The emergence of capitalism

Sociologists most commonly describe Marxist theory as a **structural–conflict** perspective. It offers a view of history that concentrates on the structures that go to make up society and considers that the dynamics of change are governed by conflict between groupings, in this case, social classes. Marx (1954) located the origins of our own form of social system, which he termed **capitalism** in the changes that emerged as a result of the Industrial and the French Revolutions. According to Marx, in pre-industrial societies, the production of both goods and services was localised and geared to the needs of the people who produced the goods. Under capitalism, production is governed by the needs of the market and by greed.

Capitalism can be identified in terms of two interrelated features:

- The production of goods and services is geared to the search for profit
- The process of production is organised in terms of a market where goods and labour power can be bought.

Capitalism is characterised by two classes:

- Those who own the means of production, whom Marx termed the **bourgeoisie**
- Those who do not own the means of production but are forced to sell their labour and to work for the bourgeoisie, whom Marx termed the **proletariat**.

The emergence of classes under capitalism

In pre-industrial societies, such as feudalism, people were forced to work unpaid for the Lord of the Manor, or to give him produce and goods. On the surface, capitalism seems a fairer system because workers sell time and skills in return for wages that can then be spent as the worker desires. In reality however, the exchange is not a fair one because the capitalist can sell goods for a far higher price than they paid the worker to make them. Wages represent less in terms of value than the value of the goods sold. The difference between these two values is kept by the bourgeoisie and in Marxist terms is known as **surplus value**, but can also be called profit. Workers work to produce goods that they cannot afford to buy and are totally dependent on the bourgeoisie for work in order to survive at a low level of subsistence. The term that Marx used to describe this condition was **wage slave**.

The development of Capitalism

Marx believed the capitalist system to be a progressive one; in this he was what is known as modernist. He saw that the introduction of labour saving machinery and sophisticated technology could make it possible for the whole population to increase their standards of living. However, the bourgeoisie did not improve the lot of the workers but kept surplus value for itself. As a result of bourgeois greed and desire for increasing amounts of profit, there was overproduction where more was being produced than could be bought. The system became unbalanced and profits fell. This allowed richer and more powerful people to buy the assets of bankrupt companies and concentrated wealth and power into the hands of the most ruthless capitalists. Marx believed that production could be centrally coordinated and orientated to people's needs, but this could never happen so long as the bourgeoisie were in competition with each other to produce profit. He believed that the solution to the problem would be a revolution organised by the proletariat. This revolution, for Marx, was inevitable, desirable and would lead to a socialist society. It is referred to by Marxists as **The Revolution** and would be prompted by a crisis of overproduction known as **the Coming Crisis of Capitalism**.

Activity
Find and read a copy of *The Communist Manifesto* (originally published 1888) by Marx and Engels. It is less difficult than you might guess, though some translations are easier than others, and it explains these processes in Marx's own words. You will benefit from reading the introduction to whichever edition you find.

The proletarians

Marx was a revolutionary. He viewed revolution as necessary and inevitable, so his analysis offers a view of a proletariat that rejects and resists bourgeois domination. He noted however, that members of the working class could struggle against each other, and saw trade unions that promoted the interests of individual groups of workers as being counter-revolutionary. He did however, look forward to a time when the proletariat would develop a class-consciousness and see itself as a unified group. They would promote the interests of the whole proletariat.

Stages in this process of developing a class-consciousness are:

- The development of capitalism means that there is a polarisation of social classes because the wealthy gain more wealth and the proletarians become poorer.
- The existence of marginalised labour is known as the **lumpenproletariat** or **reserve army of labour**, by which capitalists can keep wages low. In times of low production, these are the people who will be thrown out of work, but they can be re-employed in times of labour shortage.
- The introduction of machines means that traditional craft skills will be eroded so that divisions within the proletariat will be eliminated.

A process of class polarisation will develop in which a clearly defined and class-conscious proletariat will recognise a distinct and powerful group of bourgeoisie. As capitalism with its increasingly boom and bust economy develops through a series of crises of overproduction and economic failure, the workers will experience decrease in wages and periods of unemployment. They will be concentrated in factories and develop forms of communication that will result in organised labour movements. Eventually they will become strong enough to overthrow the capitalists and set up a new society. The process can be summarised in the following way:

- The proletariat would become larger and poorer.
- They would attain class-consciousness (awareness of the true situation of exploitation and oppression) and solidarity (work together in collective action) and become a '**class for itself**'.
- Eventually they would overthrow capitalism and attain the same relationship to the means of production (equality through communism). In this way they become a '**class in itself**'.

Sources of class power

Marx went further in his analysis of class to consider the role of the state. He pointed out that the control of the economic power of society also develops into a political domination so that the bourgeoisie become a ruling class.

The bourgeoisie maintains its power in two ways:

- **Repression and coercion**: the state owns and controls police forces and armies and these are used to control workers in industrial disputes. The state can create repressive laws that act against the interests of the people.

- **The creation of ideologies**: the bourgeoisie control the manufacture of ideas about the state, and control religious and social ideas that suggest that it is in the interests of the workers to allow the bourgeoisie to control and dominate. Workers develop a 'false consciousness' of their position in the class structure.

... the ideas of the ruling class are, in every age, the ruling ideas: if the class which is the dominant material force in society is, at the same time, its dominant intellectual force ...

Bottomore and Rubel (1961:93)

Marx hoped and believed that the Worker's Revolution would occur within his own lifetime. Over one hundred years have passed since his death and although there have been revolutions which have claimed Marx as an inspiration, none have actually fulfilled the conditions which Marx set out for the socialist revolution which would liberate workers to enjoy the fruits of their labour. This has left later writers in the Marxist tradition with the problem of finding an explanation for the failure of his prediction that the proletariat would develop class-consciousness.

An evaluation of Marxism

One of the best-known critics of Marx is Popper (1959), who writes from a rational scientific perspective and whose views are functionalist in origin. He makes the following points:

- Marxism cannot be criticised because it cannot be proved to be wrong (in any scientific sense). Marxist theory would suggest that anyone who does not agree with the ideas is suffering from 'false consciousness'.
- The Marxist theory of historical materialism accounts for societal change, which it claims, is the result of conflict between various interest groupings. According to the theory, the overthrow of capitalism is inevitable, and yet this has clearly not happened.
- Popper claims that the Communist Revolutions that have occurred have taken place because of the power of Marx's ideas and not because of historical inevitably.

He suggests that if a theory that offers a prediction cannot be falsified, it is of no value. Other criticisms of Marxist analyses of class include the suggestions that:

- Wealth has not become concentrated in the hands of fewer and fewer wealthy individuals. Wealth seems to belong to groups of individuals, corporations and companies. Think of the power of some of the multinational companies.

- Shares of companies and corporations may also belong to individuals; these individuals may belong to classes other than the bourgeoisie.
- Marxist analysis of society rests on the assumption that the owners exploit the workers, but workers can be owners themselves. Owners are difficult to identify as a separate class because some employ one or two people and others employ thousands.

However, in support of Marx, it is possible to consider the following points:

- Capitalism does retain many of the basic features outlined by Marx. There is concentration of wealth and power, particularly in the hands of men such as Rupert Murdoch, the media mogul. There is very little evidence that very much wealth has found its way downwards through the class structure. On a global level, there is increasing poverty and exploitation of the workers.
- There have been many liberal reforms in many societies and many Marxists would argue that the effect of these reforms is simply to delay the development of class-consciousness and the coming crisis of capitalism. The workers enjoy health and education benefits and even vote for their government. This gives them the illusion of participating in and benefiting from capitalism.

Activity
There are a variety of websites that offer background material on Marx and Marxism. Although some are politically motivated, others are sociological in intent and have much of interest. One of the best is at <http://www.anu.edu.au/polsci/marx/marx.html>.

MAX WEBER: ANALYSES OF CLASS

Marx was an economist and a reductionist, in that he looked for a single factor that underlies social relationships. For Marx, social class could be defined for people in terms of their relationships to the means of production. Weber saw this as essentially over simple. Weber (1985, originally published 1905) questioned Marxist emphasis on economics and saw stratification in terms of the interplay between class, status and party.

- **Status** is related to inequalities that are to do with the way in which people judge and relate to each other.
- **Class** is to do with inequalities that have their source in the workings of capitalism and the marketplace.
- **Party** is related to concepts of politics in its broadest sense. People form groups and organisations to look after their own interests.

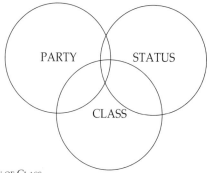

THE WEBERIAN VIEW OF CLASS

Status

Status is formed out of the tendency of people to judge each other. We all value some characteristics and despise others. When we do this as members of a social group towards members of other social categories, then we are according them a social status. Some groups will benefit from having a high status, but others may well be treated negatively. It is this key understanding which informs most debate on differentiation which follows later in this book and is an understanding that Marx failed to develop in his writing. In our society, for instance, membership of certain racial groups implies worth, so that non-membership of high status groups then disadvantages those who come from ethnic minorities. There are other status signifiers beyond ethnicity and race however. Because groups are conscious of their common status, they will follow a particular lifestyle which may or may not be consciously designed to exclude other groups and which will restrict access to membership of that group.

Status stratification for Weber does not always coincide with stratification by class. This means that even if a person acquires the wealth to belong to the highest groups in society, they may not accept that person into their social circles because they will not share values, and norms. It could be however, that if they bring their children up in a certain way, those children would have the right social as well as the correct property qualifications. Economic advantages can be used to purchase social advantages. This idea was a preoccupation of many contemporaries of Weber.

It is worth noting that just as status can confer membership of a social class on a family, the reverse is also true. The disadvantages of belonging to a low status group, such as membership of an ethnic minority, can leave people in poorly paid, low status occupations and with little hope of advancement. Weber further argued that status groups tend to gain ground and to be more significant in times of social stability, but that classes develop during periods of economic change.

Study point
If someone won a huge amount of money on the lottery, would they be able to become a member of the upper classes? What differences might there be between their culture and the culture of the richest people?

Class

It is the issue of status then which divides Marx and Weber. For Weber, class is defined as an aggregate or group of people who share a similar position in the capital market and who therefore have similar life chances. People's ability to acquire scarce resources such as health, housing and education are determined by their ability to purchase advantages in the open market. In this, Weber does not differ from Marxism in any significant way. Wealth and economic advantage are a significant element of class. However, Weber was a pluralist. This means that he believed that society is complex and in political terms, it is the role of the state to act as a disinterested arbiter between various groups. In terms of his class analysis, Weber suggested that the increasing bureaucracy which accompanies capitalism leads to status differences between those members of the working class who are manual workers and those who offer services to capitalism through the exercise of professional skills such as the middle classes. Weber suggested that there would be a growth and proliferation of classes linked to differences in educational skills and qualifications and the power that these confer on workers in the labour market. Thus, Weber rejected the Marxist concept of polarisation by identifying and explaining the growth of the middle classes. He was also able to offer an explanation for the failure of the propertyless classes to develop proletarian class-consciousness.

Table 5: *Weber's four main social classes under capitalism*	
The manual working class	Those who own nothing and sell their labour skills
The petty bourgeoisie	Those who own small businesses and are minor employers
The property-less intelligentsia	The middle classes employed by the capitalists to run and administer businesses
The propertied upper class	Those who are privileged through birth and education

Party

Weber applied the concept of power to social stratification in a different way from Marx. Weber argued that power, or the ability to exert one's will over others (with or without their consent), could derive from not only class or economic power (as Marx argued), but also from status and party. Party, or political power, can have a strong influence on social inequality and adds to the complex make-up of a person's social position. A party is a group that represents the interests of its members by influencing social policy through organised political action. There may be many different parties in a social system and they may represent the interests of a particular class, status group or neither of these. For example, in Britain New Labour can be seen as a party that represents the interests of the new affluent working class and the lower middle class, while the Green Party supports a change in policy that protects the environment and is therefore not class- or status-based.

Parties, according to Weber, support the notion of social change by enabling people's interests to be voiced. This makes the concept of party particularly important when considering the argument that social conflict has been reduced by fragmentation of social classes. If this is correct, party membership may offer one of the few routes left to challenging aspects of social inequality.

Points of evaluation

1 The main concern of a theory of class is to identify key economic and social groupings within society. By identifying a range of classes, it could be argued that Weber did not achieve this fully, but made his analysis complex and difficult for later sociologists to use as a tool of analysis.

2 Weber's theory of social stratification has been challenged for reducing the significance of social class as a way of analysing social inequality. By identifying many different classes he made it difficult to differentiate between the groups.

3 Marxists have criticised Weber for allowing status and party equal value to class in determining power. Students may like to consider the point that the nobility and aristocracy have high status in Weber's terms, but low class in that they cannot affect politics or economic events.

4 Marxists have also argued that linking social division, such as race/ethnicity and gender, to status groups, rather than class differences, ignores the genuine oppression that certain social groups experience.

5 Weber does account for the failure of the working classes to develop a sense of class-consciousness in that he allows that within a social grouping there may be considerable social mobility. However, mobility out of one social class into another one altogether is a much rarer occurrence.

Table 6: *Comparing and contrasting Max and Weber*	
MARX	WEBER
Was concerned to study the economic basis of society	Looked at a variety of institutions and their relationships
Believed that classes would polarise into two groups opposed to each other	Believed that the number of classes would proliferate (pluralism).
Failed to recognise the growth of the middle classes	Predicted the growth of the middle classes
Defined class as a collection of people who share a relationship to the means of production	Defined class as a collection of people who share the same market position
Tended to ignore the position of women and members of ethnic minorities	Failed to develop a consideration of the class position of women and members of ethnic minorities in terms of conflict with society
Recognised the significance of conflict between social groupings	Recognised the significance of conflict and competition between social groups

FUNCTIONALISM AND CLASS

Social inequality is viewed by functionalists as a way of ensuring that the most talented people receive the highest rewards in society. Power, wealth and prestige all act as motivation factors in encouraging those who can succeed to succeed. Functionalists do not discuss class divisions; instead they focus on the inevitability of social stratification as a way of maintaining a balanced society.

Parsons (1951) argued that success of social stratification was based upon primary socialisation into the norms and values of society (**value consensus**). For social inequality to be accepted, everyone must agree that it is just and worthwhile. Davis and Moore (1945) support the notion that social stratification is not only necessary, but also universal. Therefore it follows that social class acts as a way of justifying social advantage and disadvantage in a way that is acceptable to the mass of the population. In other words, the people in the highest classes (at the top end of the stratification system) are seen to represent the most talented or to be doing the most important jobs in society, which makes their higher degrees of wealth, power and prestige seem right and fair.

AN EVALUATION OF FUNCTIONALISM AND CLASS

The functionalist explanation of class inequality has been challenged for not taking into account the role of power in attaining highly rewarded positions in society. Factors such as access to different types of education (public or private), parental class position, gender, race/ethnicity, age etc can all be seen to affect one's position in the stratification system. Talent may enable some individuals to access highly rewarded occupational positions, but it does not appear to be the fundamental prerequisite.

CHANGES IN SOCIETY AND THEIR IMPACT ON CLASSIC THEORY

NEO-MARXISM AND THE RISE OF THE MIDDLE CLASSES

Marx made a clear prediction that the social classes would polarise into two opposing and competing groups. This has not happened. Instead there has been a proliferation of intermediate classes who neither own property nor survive in poverty and with poor wages. Neo-Marxists (or Marxists who adapt the work of Marx to contemporary society) support the Marxist belief that there is a basic class division between those who own the means of production and those who do not. They have, however, adapted their ideas to include the forms of paid employment that overlap boundaries between the bourgeoisie and the proletariat.

Westergaard and Resler (1976) **use** Marxism as a starting point for their analysis and point to occupation as a signifier for class because they see class as arising from people's relationship to the means of production. They distinguished three classes:

- Directors, managers, high officials and members of professions
- An intermediate cluster
- The broad mass of the ordinary people.

Therefore they acknowledge the existence of differing social experiences, but that these experiences were secondary to being members of the subject or ruling class.

Wright (1997), a neo-Marxist, argues that class conflict and the resulting social change can only be understood by categorising social class in a way that exemplifies the **contradictory class location** of certain occupations. For example, managers may appear to be middle class with a similar social experience to the ruling class, but they are actually very different, because the managers will never own the means of production and will always have links with the subject class. Therefore specific occupations may have advantages over others and allow some members of the subject class to have more power than others, such as managers over shop floor.

Wright applied an objective definition of class operationalised through occupation in relation to membership of the ruling class or subject class. His model was developed to display the way in which different occupational groups in the capitalist stratification system experience differing amounts of exploitation. He also showed how apparently 'middle class' groups could be included within the subject class.

THE CHANGING RELATIONSHIP BETWEEN THE CLASSES

During the last century and the early years of this century, it made considerable sense to see a dividing line between the manual working classes and the educated middle classes. This gap is apparent in the earliest version of the RGs Index of Social Class. Many non-manual workers are not in conflict with the manual working classes because their origins may lie in that class or because the wives and daughters of the skilled workers typically undertake lower-level non-manual work.

Parkin's (1979) solution is to base his analysis on Marxist themes in order to define classes in terms of the strategies used by groups in order to maximise rewards. He suggested that certain more powerful groups within society can restrict access to the best things in society by restricting access to resources and opportunities. They operate through tacit exclusion policies whereby only the select few have access to the rewards. This is done in capitalist society in two ways:

- Property ownership – the beneficiaries are those who own and control capital.
- Educational credentials – the beneficiaries are those who possess a monopoly of services such as lawyers and doctors.

These people can then comprise the core of the dominant classes in society. Their strategies generate conflict from the disempowered groups who then attempt to overthrow the monopoly of wealth. Parkin suggested that the resentment from the less powerful groups causes solidarity among the workers and that an example of such solidarity is the industrial strike.

According to Parkin, manual workers form the subordinate class. They attempt to usurp the power of the professional classes by imitating or by accessing the knowledge of the professional classes. The basic line of difference between the two classes for Parkin is at the point where closed and exclusive groups and the usurping groups meet each other in the class system. Certain semi-professional groups such as teachers may use both exclusion and usurpation tactics and these constitute intermediate groups between the dominant and subordinate classes.

Evaluating Parkin
However useful this view of class is in revealing tensions between particular occupational and social groupings, the attempt to define class in terms of the action of groups of people does not explain how the social groups formed initially.

NEO-WEBERIAN

Weber's analysis of the class structure in capitalist society was much more pluralistic than Marx's and therefore provided neo-Weberians (theorists who apply the work of Weber to contemporary society) with an easily adaptable framework with which to examine social stratification.

Halsey (1978), an extremely influential commentator on social class, has drawn many of his views from the work of Weber. He saw key groups in society as arising out of the way in which rewards are distributed. He distinguished three main classes:

- A professional managerial and administrative class
- An intermediate and heterogeneous class
- Manual workers.

His categories have been criticised for expanding the middle classes and for their lack of awareness of the varieties of working class groupings; however, they did form the basis of a number of studies on social class throughout the 1970s and 1980s, such as Goldthorpe's (1972) early work on social mobility.

Goldthorpe (1987) used Weber's concept of social inequality to construct a model of social class in modern capitalist societies. He identified seven classes, from the professions to agricultural workers, and attempted to explain stratification between the service, intermediate and working class through occupational status.

Goldthorpe's examination of class through occupational categories highlighted some of the differences in power that certain occupations possess. However, he has been criticised for ignoring the ruling class, not basing his classes on empirical research (which resulted in poorly defined classifications) and for ignoring the position of women in the social stratification system.

STRUCTURATION

There is a temptation to concentrate on the differences between Marxists and Weberians in their accounts of the development of class, but note that there are also similarities in their approach and their view of social class. This can best be seen in a consideration of how their theorising has been applied by more recent sociologists.

Giddens (1984) attempted to combine Marxist and Weberian explanations of class-based stratification systems in a theory known as **structuration**. Marx tended to concentrate on the ownership or non-ownership of the means of production as the main indicator of class position, while Weber focused on the market situation (occupation) of the individual to demonstrate their class. Giddens applied the Marxist notion of the social structure controlling the individual, but also used the Weberian concept of individuals being able to act independently of the social structure, thereby linking structure and action to explain social inequality. In other words, owning the means of production may allow the ruling class not to work (structure), but that they have the choice to work if they want to (action).

Runciman (1990) has put forward the proposition that class is based on a socially structured position in society, but that this position has a relative amount of power. This concept is known as **economic role** and clearly links Marxist and Weberian theory. Economic power derives from not only ownership of the means of production, but market situation and control of assets. Runciman used this notion of class to establish a model of contemporary Britain based on seven social classes, from the **upper class** owners of the means of production to the **underclass**.

AN EVALUATION OF STRUCTURATION

Both Giddens and Runciman have attempted to break through the structure versus action divide that has separated sociological thinking for so long. By examining the way in which social classes are formed, Runciman has provided a way of explaining how social structures (ownership of the means of production) and individual action (improving one's market situation) can account for class position in the occupational structure. Giddens may not have used a traditional definition of structure, but his work has encouraged sociologists to explain the divisions that exist in the class structure without the constraint of one theoretical perspective. The consequence of this has been a more thorough examination of class fragmentation, but with reference to the particular social advantages held by the upper class who remain at the top of the social stratification system.

THE NEW LEFT

Taking their philosophies broadly from the Marxist perspective, New Left theorists have offered a concept of class inequality that challenges notions of it stabilising the economy, such as those put forward by the New Right. Will Hutton (1995) has argued that social stratification not only divides society to negative effect, but that it has also had a destabilising effect on the economy. He states that class relations have been divided in three ways creating an ever-widening gap between rich and poor, in what has become known as the 30:30:40 Thesis: 30% of the population are now unemployed or in low-paid employment, 30% have some job security and 40% have secure employment. Hutton believes that this situation needs resolving, but that this can only happen when the welfare system is extended and businesses start to support the community as well as their shareholders.

EVALUATION

Hutton's thesis provides an interesting examination of class relations in modern Britain, but it has been criticised for being too structured, thereby not allowing for any overlap between, or diversity within, the three sections.

THE NEW RIGHT

The New Right can be seen to adapt the theories of functionalists in their accounts of social inequality. Peter Saunders (1995) supports the ideas of Davis and Moore (1945) in that he argues it is correct that the most talented individuals should receive the highest rewards. However, he develops this notion by examining the role of equal opportunities in ensuring that the best people for a job actually get that job.

To the New Right, equality of opportunity ensures that individual ability is rewarded, but this also means that lack of ability results in a lack of rewards. Consequently social inequality is equated with the worth of the individual to society – the people at the bottom of the stratification system are surplus to requirements. Saunders argues that this division in society encourages individuals to work hard in order to attain the best class position possible. Self-interest guides individuals in contemporary Britain and helps to maintain a stable economy.

Evaluation

Saunders has been criticised for his support of social inequality and individual self-interest for stabilising economic factors. However, he maintains that people want to achieve the highest quality of life possible and that this is the most efficient way of doing it. This said, he does acknowledge that inherited wealth can undermine notions of equality of opportunity in Britain.

Summary and Conclusion Points

Sociologists are left with deciding what exactly class should be based upon. We all know that it exists, but how do you actually describe it? How do you decide which group people belong in? This is a fundamental problem that runs throughout the context of this book. Classical sociologists have used economic indicators and power for the identification of social class.

Marxism sees class as arising out of private ownership and relationships to the means of production. He sees class as a major dynamic in the production of social change and the creation of history. Ultimately though, society will become classless as a result of the development of class-consciousness among the poorest members of society who will overthrow their oppressors. As a note of warning, do not confuse Marxism as a political system, which does not seem to have been very successful, with Marxism as an analysis of society, which is enormously influential. Weber, in his attempt to develop Marxism, by looking at other variables that can affect the class position of social groups, has created a view of a pluralistic class system with a proliferation of groups each with different aims and traditions. Although Marxism and Weberianism are in many respects, contradictory theories, when applied to the analysis of modern society, their similarities become more significant than their differences. Those who attempt to apply classical sociology to their theorising produce accounts of the class system which seem to depend on occupation, power and control for allocating class. The similarities between the two theories are further underlined when it becomes apparent that modern commentators such as **Wright (1997)** (neo Marxist) and **Giddens** (1984) (neo Weberian and structuration theorist) both consider distinctions between propertied and non-propertied and educated and uneducated to be of significance in the analysis of class.

STUDY GUIDE

Sociological Terminology exercise

Look at the following terms and be sure that you understand their meaning. Use them in your examination work:

Capitalist; Proletarian; Class-consciousness; Class for itself; Class in itself; Pluralism; Status; Party; Registrar General.

Group work

Attempt to create a class structure framework such as that created by Rose for the Registrar General (2001) that could be used to analyse class in modern Britain. What indices of class would you use to define the differences between various social groupings?

Revision hints

Stratification has always been a very significant topic for the examining boards. However, the AS/A2 split examinations will use stratification for synoptic questions rather than seeing it as a discrete topic of its own. This means that students will need to take theories of stratification and show the ability to apply them to other topics that they have studied. As a start, here is a revision and research exercise that will help you to develop your understanding of Marxist and neo-Marxist writers. To complete this research exercise, you will need to use a variety of books.

Each of the writers in the table below is associated with Marxism or neo-Marxism, or their ideas draw on and develop the themes of Marxist analysis. Find out something of what they have written and summarise their ideas in a short paragraph or so.

Table 7:	
WRITER	MAIN RESEARCH AREA
Lukes	*power*
Westergaard and Resler	*class*
Bowles and Gintis	*education*
Bordieu	*education (cultural capital)*
Althusser	*control*
Gramsci	*control and ideology*
Engels	*Family*
Hall	*media reporting of crime and deviance, also writing on class*
Oakley	*feminism and family*
Frank	*development of poor nations*
Castles and Kosack	*class and race*
Rex and Tomlinson	*ethnicity*
Illich	*health care and medicine*

Exam hints

Compare and contrast Marxist and Weberian theories of the development of class.

Evaluate the extent to which the understanding of class is central to an understanding of the structure of our society. This question allows for a variety of different approaches and you are invited to query the very significance of class analysis itself. However, given that class underlies Marxist and Weberian theory and that the work of these writers underpins the development of sociology as a discipline itself, it would be difficult to fully reject the central contention of the question without an incredibly wide range of references and knowledge. You are being invited to apply your understanding of class theory to an understanding of some of the key relationships of social structure. You could draw your examples from a wide variety of areas of sociology and society, but the framework for your answer should depend on the understanding that you have of classical theory.

Additional Reading

Wheen's new biography of **Karl Marx** (1999) London: Fourth Estate is very readable and gives a view of Marx the man.

3

WEALTH, POVERTY AND THE CLASS STRUCTURE

THIS CHAPTER IS concerned with examining analyses of the class structure of modern Britain and a consideration of the issues of social inequality – wealth, income and poverty – in our own society. Contemporary writers draw on and develop the work of the classical sociologists, but more recently the discussion has changed to encompass criticisms of the impact of government policy on the class structure and to take into account postmodern and structural analysis.

Table 8: *Theories, concepts and issues in this chapter*		
WRITERS	CONCEPTS AND CONCERNS	KEY ISSUES
Social Trends	Objective analyses of society	A number of factors affect the likelihood of people experiencing poverty.
Gordon (2000) & Pantazis (1997)	Tackling poverty	Our society is characterised by vast inequalities in wealth and power. Many people lead lives devastated by the experience of poverty.
Pantazis and Gordon (2000)	The distribution of income	There is a widening gap between rich and poor in our society.
Turak (2000) Gregg (1994)	Unemployment	Certain sectors of the workforce are more vulnerable to

		unemployment and poverty than others. Unemployment is a major cause of poverty.
Low Pay Commission (2000)	Low pay and self-employment	Many of those in employment experience poverty through poor rates of pay.
Barry (1999)	The welfare state	The welfare state was based on contradictory philosophies and so was doomed to create problems for itself.
Murray (1984)	The New Right	The Welfare State creates dependency and an underclass.
Davis and Moore (1967)	Functionalism	Poverty is necessary for society to function effectively.
Conflict perspectives	Society is organised to benefit the rich and powerful	Is social inequality inevitable?
Pahl and Wallace (1988)	Postmodernism	Class is an irrelevant concept.

WEALTH, INCOME AND LIFE CHANCE

Table 9: *Differences between income and wealth*	
INCOME	WEALTH
Income is money which comes in at regular intervals	Wealth includes assets such as savings and investments
Income helps people to buy goods	Wealth offers long-term security and status
Income is money	Wealth can be converted to money if sold
Income can be invested to become wealth	Wealth can be used to create a regular income through interest on savings accounts and pension plans
Income can be related to employment and therefore is vulnerable to changes in the market	Much wealth is acquired through inheritance and not earnings

WEALTH

Wealth refers to assets that are surplus to a person's requirement and exists over and above income. It can take the form of property which can be sold to create money and which is not immediately needed by the person owning it: stocks, bonds, shares, paintings, jewellery, property and land. Much wealth is held in the form of savings, as investments and in pension plans.

There are three routes to becoming wealthy:

- Through inheritance of money, land and property eg The Duke of Westminster owns 138,000 acres of land, much of it in the expensive parts of London
- Through success in business eg Richard Branson or the Guinness family
- Through success in art, sport, leisure or popular culture eg Sir Paul McCartney or Michael Owen.

Table 10: *Difficulties in obtaining accurate data on wealth*
• Problem in defining wealth eg marketable assets (savings, property, stocks and shares) and/or non-marketable wealth (state pensions, occupational pensions).
• Fluctuations in asset values.
• Wealth statistics are mainly taken from estate tax returns, which tend to be inaccurate; eg tax-avoidance strategies may be employed by the wealthy, such as making 'gifts' to relatives.
• People may invest their wealth overseas.

INCOME

This is money or benefits that comes into a household. It can be earned in the form of a wage (earned) or it can be interest on wealth (unearned) or can take the form of state benefits. People may have a high income and yet have little wealth so that if they were to lose their jobs, they would then have little money on which to live.

According to Marxist sociologists Westergaard and Resler (1975) government taxation on income has had little redistributive effect on levels of wealth. Money has not been taken from the rich and given to the poor, because there are so many concessions given to high earners, such as reductions on insurance policies and pensions. Also, it appears that the provisions of the welfare state are utilised more frequently and effectively by the non-poor, for example medical services and schooling.

Activity
Classify the following as either income or wealth: holiday home, pension plan, interest from savings account, earnings from a job, rental income from a flat you own, investments, artwork, jewellery, stocks and shares, land, social security benefits.

LIFE CHANCES

This refers to the opportunities that people have in their lives: their chances of higher education for instance or their chances of obtaining high-paid work. People in lower-income brackets tend to have fewer life chances than those in the non manual social classes.

There is a clear link between a person's social class and the opportunities or life chances that they may experience. This has been shown by a number of government surveys and sociological studies into the population of Britain. People in the lower classes of the Registrar General's Index of Social Class earn less, live shorter and less healthy lives, experience higher disability, divorce and criminal conviction rates and are more likely to die in poverty than those people who were born into non-manual families. As Wilkinson (1996) identified, people at the bottom of the stratification system in Britain have severely-reduced life chances:

In Britain people in the poorest areas have death rates that are – age for age – four times as high as people in the richest areas. Among Whitehall civil servants junior staff were found to have death rates three times as high as the most senior administrators working in the same offices.

THE DEMOGRAPHIC FEATURES OF POVERTY

Demography is the study of populations. The best sources of information on the population come from statistical data collected annually by the government as part of their planning and policy making and published as part of the *Social Trends* series.

- *Age* – there is a clear link between membership of certain age groups and poverty. Dependence on an old age pension for sole income, for instance, means that people survive on limited means. Families become vulnerable to poverty when the children are young.
- *Locality* – regions that experience poverty are likely to be on the periphery of Britain and away from the economically productive South and Midlands. The

New Earnings Survey of 1995 identified that average weekly wages varied by nearly £30 with male manual workers in the south-east earning £310.70 and those in Wales earning £284.40 per week.

- *Gender* – females are particularly vulnerable to poverty. They make up the bulk of single parents and they tend to live longer than males. This means that many females are benefit dependent. Also, women who are in employment tend to suffer from lower pay and poorer conditions than men.
- *Ethnicity* – certain ethnic groups are particularly susceptible to long term unemployment. **Champion** et al (1996) point out that where unemployment is high among whites, then it is likely to be much higher again for non-whites in many areas of the country, particularly in those with a high proportion of non-whites in the population. **Sly** (1994) claimed that ethnic minority groups suffered unemployment at rates that were double those for the white population.
- *Family structure* – **Social Trends** (1992) suggests those children at particular risk of poverty live in single parent households.

Study point

Develop your knowledge by collecting data from *Social Trends* and other government sponsored books which you can find in any good library.

THE DISTRIBUTION OF INCOME

There are some areas to consider in any debate on the relationship between income and stratification. They are respectively:

- Wealth and inequalities in contemporary Britain
- Employment and income
- The role of the welfare state and social inequalities.

WEALTH AND INEQUALITIES IN CONTEMPORARY BRITAIN

If one takes an overview of our society, the economy seems to be healthy. Compared to many countries around the world, Britain is relatively affluent and living standards for the general population are high and have never been better. Some sections of society have seen a very steady rise in income over the years. However, all is not as it seems and one major result of the policies of the New Right and of Thatcherism was to increase the pay differential between the highest- and the lowest-earning people in our society. **Gordon** (2000) quoting statistics gathered by the Department of Social Security notes that the richest 10% of the population have increased their share of income from 20% to 28% between

1979 and 1996. At the same time, the poor were not only relatively poorer because they owned fewer of the things deemed necessary for an acceptable standard of living, but they were actually much poorer in financial terms after taking account of rises in prices. This analysis, which shows a widening gap between the earnings of the wealthiest and the poorest, is supported by the findings of the Low Pay Commission.

THE POOR

Many sectors of the workforce have seen no real rise in income and many have become unemployed. It is argued that an increasing proportion of those who survive on low pay or benefit are falling below the poverty line. Gordon and Pantazis (1997) suggest that between 1983 and 1990 there was a 50% increase in poverty with a rise from 14% to 20% (11 million people) of households living below socially acceptable standards of living. One fifth of the population of Britain live lives that are characterised by the following symptoms of poverty:

- Poor and unheated housing
- Lack of essential clothing
- Poor or inadequate nutrition
- Lack of household goods such as carpet, fridge, telephone
- Social isolation and depression
- Fear of crime
- Serious illness.

The poorest 10% of the population only have around 3% of the total income, less than a third of what they would have if income were equally distributed … The richest 30% have well over half of all income between them while the richest 10% alone receive over a quarter of all income.

The shares of income that various groups have tell us about their control over resources.

Goodman, Johnson and Webb (1997:63)

THE WEALTHY

In contrast, it is difficult to find out about the actual wealth of certain individuals in our society. The Inland Revenue acknowledges that it does not have accurate data. Journalists on *The Sunday Times* produce a **Rich List** annually, but note the limits of their methods in discovering how much people really own. In 1996, they estimated that the wealthiest 500 people owned assets totalling £70.58 billion. The top 20 in the list owned £22.78 billion and the top 300 had wealth totalling £62.20 billion. Many of these individual people had wealth in excess of some of the world's least wealthy countries.

Pantazis and Gordon (2000) suggest that the wealthiest 1,000 people own two thirds as much as the poorest 50% of the population and that the 'richest 1,000 had on average 15,000 times more wealth than the least wealthy 28 million'. They go on to comment on the political and democratic dimensions of such inequality of access to wealth.

Problems of acquiring accurate data on wealth
* It is difficult to provide an agreed definition of wealth.
* Some property varies in value depending on the market.
* The statistics are based on tax returns.
* There are many tax avoidance strategies such as deeding and gifting property to dependants.
* People may own overseas investments.
* One's position in the life course may alter. An individual with young children will be significantly less wealthy than one who is living alone and with no dependants.

EMPLOYMENT AND INCOME

The structure of the British economy has undergone radical change since the end of the Second World War. There has been a massive move away from employment in primary industries, those involved in the production of raw materials such as agriculture and coal mining. Manufacturing or secondary industry has also experienced a drop in employment. There has been a reduction in traditionally male heavy industry and a growth in light industry and assembly work that can be automated and which employs more females. The real growth sector in the economy has been in service sector jobs. Many of these are middle class jobs in management and training, however, more are jobs which offer long hours, low pay and casual part time work in restaurants and pubs. These changes have had a very significant impact on the study of stratification in Britain and provide a theme for much of the remainder of this text.

Turak (2000) points out that the actual number of manual jobs has fallen by 11% between 1981 and 1991 while non-manual jobs have expanded. Certain sectors of the workforce have been more vulnerable to unemployment, and he points to the older male manual worker as being particularly vulnerable. **Gregg** (1994) has claimed that one of the main causes of poverty in Britain is unemployment and that Britain had a third more families out of work than other developed countries. Statistics suggest that in a fifth of households, there is no adult in employment and although in the rest of Europe, 80% of single parents work, in Britain the figure is closer to 40% of single parents in work.

Summary of points
* There has been a decrease in manual work in Britain since the 1970s and an increase in non-manual work.

IN THE 1930s, IT WOULD HAVE BEEN COMMON TO SEE MALES EMPLOYED IN PRIMARY INDUSTRY OR HEAVY INDUSTRIAL MANUFACTURING, BUT INCREASINGLY FEWER PEOPLE ARE ENGAGED IN SUCH WORK AND THIS TYPE OF PHOTOGRAPH HAS BECOME SYMBOLIC OF THE PAST.

- Women are now a more significant part of the workforce but their labour tends to be part-time and low paid.
- There has been an increase in unemployment especially among certain social groupings.
- Income differentials between the highest- and the lowest-paid workers in the economy have become increasingly wide.

THE LOW PAID

In 1994, it was established that 2.2 million workers in Britain earned less than 68% of the average gross weekly wage that stood at less than £6.00 per hour in that year. These low paid workers tended to be female, the young, the disabled, single parents and members of ethnic minorities. Their work was part-time, homework or casual labour and they tended to be found in certain areas, and in smaller firms. Evidence presented to the Low Pay Commission by the Greater Manchester Low Pay Unit (2000) described one woman who had taken on three low-paid jobs at one time in order to 'make ends meet'.

THE MINIMUM WAGE

Minimum wage legislation was introduced by the Labour government with effect from April 1999 and is currently set at £3.60. Early in 2000, a number of Labour Party MPs and trade unionists requested that there should be annual upgrading of the minimum wage by the 10p an hour recommended by the Low Pay Unit. They also sought the lowering of the adult rate to the age of 21 rather than 22. They argued that the government is overcautious and too attentive to extensive lobbying from employers' organisations. Employers' organisations had predicted a massive increase in unemployment following the introduction of a minimum wage, but this did not occur. Michael Portillo, the Conservative shadow chancellor, announced in February 2000 that the Conservatives now supported the principle of a minimum wage.

Activity
You are strongly advised to look at the website of the Low Pay Commission at *http://www.lowpay.gov.uk/* . It offers an extensive list of press releases and study reports. Much of the data in this chapter is drawn from this work.

SELF-EMPLOYMENT INCOME

Self-employment was not a popular option in Britain until the 1980s, when the number of people being self-employed rose by nearly half. This meant that by the early 1990s over 10% of the people in work were responsible for generating their own incomes. It also fostered the belief that the petit bourgeoisie, or middle class, was expanding in modern Britain.

Recent governments, particularly the last Conservative government, have declared themselves keen to support self-employment, based on ideas of private enterprise developing structural differentiation. This positive concept of self-employment has been supported by the arguments of writers such as Carrington, McCue and Pierce (1995) who suggest that self-employed workers are less likely to be affected by changes in the employment market and by wages cycles. Increased levels of self-employment may also be seen to support the idea that 'we are all middle class now', suggesting that levels of wealth and income have increased to make us all more affluent.

Neo-Marxists, however, have suggested that self-employment has simply acted as an alternative to unemployment. The proletariat worker has not changed, only the structure of their labour. Self-employment is useful to the government, because it acts as a reserve pool for labour, as well as reinforcing the benefits of capitalist entrepreneurialism (potential wealth and autonomy) to the masses. Self-employment is therefore not a signal for the expansion of the middle class, but rather a sign of a restructured labour market.

Robson (1999) has suggested that there are significant regional variations in the rate of self-employment among British males. For the period 1973–93, he discovered that regional rates of self-employment are linked to the real value of housing wealth, and therefore the economic health of the region. Other factors involved are linked with the support for self-employment and infrastructure of the region itself.

Champion et al (1996) point out that certain ethnic groups are far more likely to be self-employed than others. The Chinese are the highest in this group, and Indians and Pakistanis follow them. Bangladeshi families are also more likely to be self-employed than the white population. However, as Savage et al (1992) point out self-employment is also an option taken by managers as an attempt to realise their assets, assets that cannot be passed on through inheritance whilst working for an employer. Managers, black or white, may be an asset to a particular company or organisation, but this asset is hard to transfer or realise. Becoming self-employed may remove the problem of access to assets, enabling the manager to reap the benefits of their hard work.

THE ROLE OF THE WELFARE STATE IN SOCIAL INEQUALITIES

It is important to study state policy with regard to taxation and benefit, because it is through state policy that income can be redistributed towards the poor via higher taxation and benefit levels, or it can be retained by the wealthy through low taxation and reduced benefits.

DISTRIBUTION AND REDISTRIBUTIONISM

Barry (1999) argues that the growth in the idea that the government should involve itself in health and welfare was a twentieth-century idea prompted by the mass unemployment of the 1930s and the belief that only government action could relieve the problem. It became clear to politicians at that time that unemployment was not an issue of personal laziness but created by economic factors beyond the individual control of workers.

- *Distributionism* – the idea that wealth is distributed through the economy according to productivity.
- *Redistributionism* – money should be distributed through the economy according to need. This is a philosophical position based on a value judgement that poverty is 'wrong'. This is a view traditionally associated with leftwing and liberal political positions.

The Beveridge Report of 1942 suggested that it was the role of the state to provide through various forms of taxation. Individuals paid into insurance schemes and these then offered support through times of poverty. The weakness of such thinking is that there is no limit defined for neediness and with relative definitions of poverty in operation, need will continue to increase as the general standard of living increases, thus increasing the burden on those in work to pay for those who do not work. As an example, those who designed the National Health Service could not have predicted the improvement in medical technology over the last 55 years, nor its cost. Related to this discussion, there is another series of debates (Le Grand, 1982) concerned with the question of who actually pays into redistributive schemes, and who benefits.

- Do the poor pay proportionally more of their income into health and welfare schemes than the rich? There is a case to argue that the welfare state is more of a burden for the poor in employment than the wealthy.
- Do wealthier people benefit more than the poor from state welfare and support systems such as education schemes? There is much evidence to suggest that they do.

Thus (Le Grand, 1982) argues that the poorest members of society do not benefit from the welfare state as much as those in the middle classes.

It was this set of problems which lay at the heart of New Right thinking on economics and the state. Taking their position from pluralism and functionalism, Conservative politicians and thinkers of the 1980s emphasised individual responsibilities and the loosening of dependence on the state. Many New Right thinkers, such as **Marsland** (1989) and **Murray** (1984) suggested that it was the existence of the welfare state which created poverty through the creation of a culture of dependency and the development of an underclass of benefit claimants. There was also a belief that taxation is unpopular with voters. Much taxation became indirect so that VAT was increased, but successive Chancellors of the Exchequer reduced direct taxation. The impact of this type of ideology and theorising was that a series of budgets reduced taxation and that benefits became more difficult to claim or were means tested.

Social security and taxation policies provided the most direct means for the Thatcher governments to reward the rich while making the poor poorer. Under Thatcher there were substantial reductions in income tax for people living on higher incomes, particularly in the 1980 and the 1988 Budgets. Nigel Lawson's 1988 'give away' budget, which reduced the top rate of income tax from 60 to 40%, resulted in £2 billion in tax going to the richest 5% of the population.

Pantazis and Gordon (2000:5)

The 1997 Labour government of Tony Blair, has promised to reduce poverty and was widely reported as saying that if poverty were not reduced, then the government would not deserve re-election. Chancellor Gordon Brown promised to take one million children out of poverty by 2001. There have been increases in universal child benefit and a series of measures designed to target families on low wages, such as the Working Families Tax Credit and the Children's Tax Credit. It is argued that these will have the biggest effect on poverty. The Labour Party claims that by the year 2002 these policies will target an extra £4 billion at families with children, taking 800,000 children and 550,000 parents out of poverty. Note that the Labour Party has made fewer claims about reducing social inequality.

Study point
Organise a discussion to the question: is it possible to reduce poverty without tackling social inequality in society?

RELATING THEORY TO REALITY

FUNCTIONALISM AND SOCIAL INEQUALITY

Operating from a consensus perspective, functionalists such as Davis and Moore (1967) are tied to the view that poverty is necessary for the health of society. People are not born with equal abilities and society is organised to ensure that the best and most worthy people will be rewarded for their contribution to the good of society. Inequality is a way of allocating scarce resources, allows people to feel motivated to improve their position in society and it gives the wealthy the opportunity to help the poorest and to govern society to benefit everyone else.

Points of evaluation
- From an educational perspective, many research studies have suggested that success is not related to intelligence or ability but to the social class of parents. In particular, **Halsey** (1980) showed, in his study of **Oxford Mobility**, that there was a link between class and educational attainment in Britain.
- Tumin (1967) argued that underachievement among the poorer sectors of society results in alienation and waste of talent.
- It is clear that wealth is not redistributed among all classes. The middle strata of society may have become wealthier as a result of Thatcherism, but the poorest sectors of society still control a very small proportion of the total wealth of the country.

CONFLICT PERSPECTIVES

This perspective offers the view that people are born unequal in ability, but that these inequalities are of no real social significance and do not offer an explanation for the vast inequalities which we see in our society. Society is organised to benefit the wealthy and the powerful at the expense of the weak and the powerless. The wealthy and powerful use ideological weapons to control the powerless and offer a misleading view of the world that can blind them to their true interests. For example, Marxists argue that the proletariat are ideologically conditioned into accepting their oppression by the bourgeoisie. Feminists argue that women and men are socialised into seeing their gender roles as appropriate and therefore do not challenge them. Overall, conflict perspectives suggest that those people in society who lack wealth and income and have poor life chances are the ones who have limited access to scarce resources, based upon a socially constructed stratification system.

Points of evaluation
- Societies that claim to have followed Marxist principles have been as unequal, if not more so, as capitalist societies. Many European states based on the principles of Marxism have now abandoned the social concept and are adopting more openly inequitable systems based on mixed economies, which unite capitalism and communism.
- It is difficult for writers to claim that certain social groupings, such as the working class, women or ethnic minorities share a social class if there are large inequalities of wealth and income within these groups.

POSTMODERNISM AND SOCIAL STRATIFICATION

Pahl and Wallace (1988) have rejected classic Marxist and Weberian theories of social class on the basis that they represent the concerns and society of the nineteenth century and have no relevance to modern society. They accept postmodern analyses of society and see inequality as an issue of the ability to purchase commodities, and not as an issue of identity or social status. Many working class people can afford to purchase luxury items and may well own their own homes. The weakness of their view is that they ignore inequality of ownership of wealth and could therefore be argued as offering an over-optimistic analysis.

Summary and Conclusion
British society has been characterised by increasing differences between wealth and poverty over the past twenty years. There has been an increase in the numbers of people experiencing unemployment and dependency on welfare payments; these tend to be certain social groups such as women, the disabled and members of non-white ethnic minorities. There are two views of the impact of this on the economy of the country.

1 The government is subsidising employers who are underpaying certain sectors of the community.
2 The burden of certain sectors of the community on tax payers has increased and should be reduced.

Equally, at the same time, there has been a rise in the influence and wealth of the middle and higher sectors of society so that social inequalities are more obvious and widespread than they have been for many years. Has this given rise to a situation where traditional explanations of class are no longer significant? Is it possible that although class is no longer as clearly understood and signposted by many, as it was in the times of the classic theorists, it still has a relevance to an understanding of the structure of inequality in our society? Although politicians of the Right such as Thatcher and John Major choose to disregard class in their analyses, it is still one of the most significant social creations affecting the lifestyles and life chances of people in modern Britain. Postmodernists and New Labour may seem to many to underplay the significance of the impact of poverty on lifestyle among the working class in a modern capitalist society, but social policy makers must understand this if they want to examine the causes and consequences of social stratification and differentiation. It is therefore possible for the New Right and some of the New Left to view the poor as the agents of their own misfortune.

STUDY GUIDE

Sociological Terminology exercise

Look at the following terms and be sure that you understand their meaning. Use them in your examination work:

Income; Wealth; Property; Inequality; Poverty; Distribution and redistribution.

Group work

Organise a discussion to the suggestion that poverty does not exist in the advanced industrial societies.

You will need to ensure that your group has done plenty of research on poverty and inequality in Britain. You will need to be certain that you understand that poverty has two meanings: objective poverty refers to a lack of things which are essential for life and relative poverty refers to a lack of the things that others deem necessary for an acceptable standard of living.

Compare and contrast two areas of your town and see the relationship between life chances and social class.
- Which areas are pleasanter to live in? (Think about access to parks, shops, leisure facilities, quality of life.)
- Look at the local estate agents and newspapers to compare the prices and values of the houses in the various areas of town.
- Look at the various housing areas and decide as far as it is possible how much money you might need to buy some of the houses in the attractive areas of town. Which social classes tend to live in these various areas, do you think?

Revision hints

Good sources of information to develop the notes which you have been given by your teacher include various government publications such as *Social Trends*. You may wish to visit the website of the Joseph Rowntree Foundation at *<http://www.jrf.org.uk/jrf.html>*. Look for political groups in other countries which campaign on behalf of the socially disadvantaged. Charities for the poor are less useful to you because they are unlikely to have a campaigning agenda. They rely on governments and official bodies for support and therefore cannot easily take the risk of offending potential patrons.

Exam hints

Evaluate the suggestion that inequality is functional and necessary for our society.

You will need to identify the suggestion as a structural–functional view in your analysis of the question. It would be tempting for students to dismiss the functionalist view out of hand as many people take a moralistic stance on inequality in our society. The essay will be better for an explanation of why functionalism is tolerant and accepting of inequality, especially if it focuses on the work of classical sociologists such as Durkheim. This is an easy way to explore and display knowledge of social theory. You will also need to explain the link between functionalist theorising and the policies of the New Right which were tolerant of inequality and which practised financial policies that had the effect of increasing the gap between the richest and the poorest in Britain throughout the 1980s and early 1990s.

Those who are poor are likely to be a financial burden on the state and to become part of a pool of talent and ability that is wasted. Can a modern state afford to have a population which is poor, alienated and disaffected? The evaluation remains your own, but to gain the marks you will need to explore both sides of the issue.

4

CLASS, FRAGMENTATION AND CONTEMPORARY SOCIETY

THIS CHAPTER IS concerned with the examination of accounts of the class structure of modern Britain with reference to the nature of individual class groupings that have been identified by theorists. The analyses of class which sociologists are now using to understand British culture are drawn from the understandings which you should bring to the discussion from your reading in Chapters One and Two. Both Marx and Weber have been extremely influential on modern writers and analyses of class, but there has also been an important recent contribution to the debate from those working from a postmodern perspective.

Table 11: *Tseories, concepts and issues in this chapter*		
WRITERS	CONCEPTS/CONCERNS	KEY ISSUES
Scott (1982, 1986)	Neo-Marxist	Upper class combined landowners with capitalists
Miliband (1973) Westergaard and Resler (1975)	Marxism	There is a unified upper class
Dahrendorf (1959)	Weberian	Wealth rests in the hands of corporations
Adonis and Pollard (1998)	Superclass	Is there an emerging 'superclass' in Britain?
Gramsci (1971)	Neo-Marxist	Hegemony and capitalism

Wright Mills (1956) Edgell (1993) Millerson (1964)	The middle classes	Who are the middle classes?
Braverman (1974)	Neo-Marxist	The proletarianisation of the professions
Savage et al (1992)	Middle-class lifestyles	There are three separate forms of middle class lifestyle
Marx (1867)	Working class	The working class as an oppressed revolutionary mass
Goldthorpe et al (1968) Devine (1992)	Embourgeoisement	Is it possible for affluent workers to become middle class?
Crewe (1992)	Partisan dealignment thesis	The emergence of a new working class
Dahrendorf (1992)	Fragmented working class	There are three layers to the working class
Pahl (1984)	Divided working class	Decomposition of the working class is based on the collapse of the manufacturing industries
Murray (1982)	New Right	The underclass as an undesirable mass.
Giddens (1973) Brown and Madge (1982)	Leftwing	Underclass as the weakest members of society
Runciman (1990)	Reconciling Marxism and Weberianism	British society can be explained based on a seven class model
Giddens (1984)	Structuration	Society and people affect each other via globalisation
Lash and Urry (1987)	Postmodernism	The end of social class?

THE UPPER CLASS

Much written political and social history is actually the history of the wealthy and influential. It was really only in this century that historians began to try and understand the development of the poorer and illiterate sections of the community. In contrast, sociology has a huge amount of data on those we may consider to be working class, but there have been fewer analyses of the very wealthy. In this section it is necessary to consider the importance and significance of the wealthy within the class structure, because it is the group that has the most advantages in the social stratification system.

THE ORIGINS OF THE UPPER CLASSES

The great aristocratic and land-owning families in Britain tend to be descended from the knights and warlords of feudal society. Great families jostled with each other for supremacy in a series of wars. The emergence of modern society in Tudor times saw the same wars continue, only the battleground changed to the political arena and the weapons were religion, politics, law and financial control of the state. It was at the time of the English Civil War that a more settled aristocracy developed into a gentrified class that we would recognise as a unified social grouping.

SCOTT AND THE UNIFICATION OF THE UPPER CLASS THESIS

Scott (1982, 1986), a neo-Marxist, argues that membership of the dominant classes emerged from the ownership of land and the income and wealth derived from that land. He suggests that there were two upper classes in pre-industrial society, the **landed magnates** who owned vast estates and the **landed gentry** who farmed smaller units of land. With the development of the changes that took place in society during the early Industrial Revolution, two more classes emerged: a financial and commercial upper class and a manufacturing class who appear from the origins of capitalistic class described by Marx.

According to Scott, late in the nineteenth century, there was intermarriage between these groups so that wealthy businessmen gained status by marrying their children into the impoverished aristocracy. There was an exchange of money for social status and Scott claims the three classes were unified into one business class at the turn of the twentieth century that developed from the merging of social and class interests.

Scott sees the upper class as consisting of three groups who have shared but slightly differing interests:

- **Entrepreneurial capitalists** who invest money in businesses
- **Internal capitalists** who work for companies

- **Finance capitalists** who draw their wealth from a variety of business interests and directorships.

Because of their merged and familial interests, this group of people are able to control economic and political power within the state.

Points of evaluation
Scott takes account of pluralistic criticisms of Marxism that make the following points:

- Not all capitalists are politicians.
- Not all politicians necessarily come from capitalistic classes.

Criticisms of Scott can be based on his debatable historical analysis and his insistence on a divided dominant class within the nineteenth century.

- Early venture capitalists often purchased land and estates in order to gain social respectability and credibility throughout the industrial period. Many estates in Avon and Gloucestershire are based on mercantile colonial interests, particularly slavery.
- The Butes who are associated with South Wales and the industrial development of Cardiff were aristocratic, wealth was based on mineral extraction from lands they owned and on the profits from exploitative coalmining, docking, shipping and slum developments.

Study point
Visit some of the great houses in your own neighbourhood and then find out something of the family history. Do you see evidence of colonial, military or business interests in their possessions and interests?

CLASSICAL MARXIST ANALYSES

One of the most notable writers on the issue of class was Miliband (1973) who argued that economic and political power are closely linked. His ideas are linked with the notion of the upper class as an 'Establishment' and he takes the view that there is a unified upper class. Individuals, because of their class position, are able to take jobs where they are able to exercise power, such as in the civil service. They are able to maintain their class position through their ability to influence state decision-making. The state itself becomes an agency of class power. It is the idea of a unified dominant class that Scott is criticising; however, rather than rejecting Miliband, his intention is to open the debate within the Marxist perspective.

Westergaard and Resler (1975) produced a classic and detailed Marxist study
that makes a strong argument for a unified and dominant upper class united by
interests of wealth and power. Those who are managers of major companies are
also shareholders. Further, they claim that these people comprise between 5 and
10% of the British population.

DAHRENDORF AND THE 'DECOMPOSITION OF CAPITAL'

Dahrendorf (1959) takes a pluralistic stance. His theorising is based on
Weberianism and therefore takes account of the role of the individual as well as
of the social structure. He notes that although individual businesspeople do own
and control wealth and share capital, the real wealth is concentrated in the hands
of corporations. These corporations operate according to the rules of social
organisations and cannot therefore be the individual tools of powerful people.
They are responsible to the needs of the market, shareholders and the politicians
of the countries where they are located. This limits their freedom to operate as
freestanding concerns.

Capitalists and managers have conflicting interests and the upper class is
therefore limited in its power to influence events of the state because it is
decomposing; individual members have separate interests. This position
provides a starting point for some postmodern and New Right analyses of the
upper classes, which suggest that the upper classes are fragmenting and are not
significant because they require highly paid managers to actually run the
businesses which they own. This process is known as the **managerial revolution**
and is associated with the ideas of **Saunders**, a prominent New Right
theoretician.

THE DEVELOPMENT OF A NEW SUPERCLASS?

Recent work by Adonis and Pollard (1998) stresses the significance of the upper
class in modern British society and they consider that there is an emerging
'superclass' that consist of an elite of extremely high-paid managers and
professionals. According to Adonis and Pollard, the superclass is linked
financially to the City of London, a male and upper class world that has many

links with the traditions and heritage of public school and Oxbridge elites of the past. This superclass emerged from the financial upheavals of the 1980s and is composed of people who benefited from low taxation and privatisation of industry to become significant in international trading with global companies.

Adonis and Pollard suggest that the superclass are frequently members of the old dominant or land-owning upper classes who have become absorbed into financial careers and benefit from investing their money in City trading. They no longer belong to a tradition of service to state, empire or community as members of the upper classes would once have been and the implication is that they have become self-regarding in their attitudes. They justify their high earnings and high status by using meritocratic arguments and referring to their education, values and lifestyle. However, they are divorced from the reality of life in modern British society, protected as they are by their wealth, investment and income.

Activity
Look at the business sections of the important Sunday newspapers such as *The Observer* and *The Sunday Times*. Look at copies of *The Financial Times*. Find profiles of prominent business people and see if their salaries are mentioned. What particular character traits do they bring to their work? Did any originate from what may be described as traditional working class backgrounds?
To what extent do these people fit the model of an elite of highly paid managers and controllers?

THE MIDDLE CLASSES

There is a very strong argument to suggest that the middle classes are a historical development arising out of the needs of the industrial revolution for a management elite and the decline of the significance of the Church in controlling literacy and numeracy. The most significant problem for sociologists however, is how to define the middle class – there are considerable variations of wealth and status within the groups who are not wealthy or powerful enough to be described as dominant and yet who do not work with their hands. The importance for the theoretical sociologist is that the development of the middle class is a test of Marxism in the sense that Marx predicted a polarisation of classes with extremes of wealth and poverty, but in fact, the pattern seems to be one of a proliferation and fragmentation of classes in the centre of the social spectrum.

MARX, WEBER AND THE DEATH OF THE MIDDLE CLASSES

In the middle of the last century, the middle classes were seen as those who owned the means of production but who worked for themselves in small businesses. Marx argued that the middle classes would be absorbed into the ranks of the proletariat as the wealth and power of the plutocrats or capitalistic classes was concentrated into fewer hands. Weber, as a pluralist, predicted an expansion of the number of classes and he saw the middle classes as ensuring that they gained more wealth, status and power for themselves through the acquisition of skills, hence they would be absorbed into the upper classes.

GRAMSCI AND THE INTELLECTUALS

Gramsci (1971) was not concerned with the development of class so much as to consider the nature and maintenance of power. His great contribution to sociology was probably the concept of the **bourgeois hegemony**, which outlined the methods used by the capitalist classes to control the values and morality of society. Linked to this is his consideration of the role of the intellectual in the state, and this is of particular relevance to the question of social strata and the development of the middle classes in society. He claimed that capitalism required the presence of intellectuals who could serve the interests of the ruling classes.

- **Traditional intellectuals** – these are the educated people, the philosophers and professors. They are a conservative group who serve the ruling classes through the creation of ideas.
- **Organic intellectuals** – these are created by the education system to run the institutions of the state for the bourgeoisie. Gramsci wanted the working classes to develop their own organic intellectuals who could counter the role of the state and create a sense of class-consciousness.

FORMS OF THE MIDDLE CLASS

Wright Mills (1956) identified two separate elements of the middle class which form the basis of much of the following sociological debate.

- 'Old' middle class – property-owning
- 'New' middle class – property-less professionals enjoying wealth through earning potential and education.

THE PROPERTIED MIDDLE CLASSES

These are the middle classes that merge into the upper class, a group whom Marx identified as the petty bourgeoisie and whom he predicted would lose their class position as capitalism developed. Edgell (1993) suggests that there are three forms of theorising associated with the development of this class:

- **The demise thesis** suggests that this class will disappear. Edgell suggests that this class is composed of the self-employed who protect themselves from redundancy.
- **Marginalisation thesis** suggests that the old middle classes are marginalised in modern society and are of little significance, providing a refuge for those who become unemployed until they can be reabsorbed into the workplace.
- **Demarginalisation thesis** suggests that the petit bourgeoisie will develop and expand because they provide support services for capitalism in the form of labour-intensive business, based on information technology and ethical principles and which are meritocratic in that good businesses will prosper.

THE PROFESSIONAL MIDDLE CLASSES

There has been a vast area of debate surrounding the position of the property-less middle classes because they represent one of the fastest growing sectors of the labour market. Wright Mills (1956) claimed that the professions were the servants of the wealthy and powerful, and talked of the development of a power elite among this group who wield influence on behalf of their employers. Most commentators divide this professional class into two groups:

- **The higher professionals** who have the potential for high earnings and who may be self-employed or employed by large corporations – judges, accountants, lawyers, dentists, doctors. These people tend to control entry into their occupations.
- **The lower professionals** who are often, though not exclusively, feminised and who work in the public domain and have limited access to high earnings – teachers, nurses, social workers. Entry to these professions is open.

Millerson (1964) offered a very positive view of professions in attempting to create a model of their characteristics:

- Skills based on theory
- Skills based on practice
- Skills based on proven competencies
- Integrity
- Public service
- Organised and self-regulatory.

PROLETARIANISATION THESIS AND THE DESKILLING OF PROFESSIONS

Marxists, such as Braverman (1974) offer a different view of the professions arguing instead that as professionals have become employees, they have lost their independence of action and of power. Many of the professionals, such as architects, have become vulnerable to redundancies. Others, such as teachers or opticians, being unable to control entry into their professions are no longer able to claim high rates of pay as there is always demand for work and people who are willing to accept low rates in return for employment. **Oppenheimer** (1973) has taken these views a step further and suggests that many professionals, such as welfare administrators, have become tools of control for the state in the administration of scarce public resources.

Points of evaluation
- Although some sectors of the middle class have experienced a drop in status and job security, their conditions of service and their pay remain significantly better than those of the working class.
- Certain professions, particularly accountancy, are expected to put their employer before their professional ethics.
- It is possible that certain feminised professions such as office and clerical work have become proletarianised in that they have become deskilled and workers have little autonomy over their work. Other professions however, retain power and autonomy.

THE MIDDLE CLASSES AND LIFESTYLE CHOICE

Savage et al (1992) have developed the fragmentation debate in order to identify a model of three separate forms of middle class lifestyle that may overlap slightly in some individuals.

- **Postmodern** – these are the high earning professional middle class who have considerable disposable income which will be spent on high value consumer goods. They combine this with a highly disciplined personal style which emphasises health and body consciousness.
- **Ascetic** – these are the highly educated low earners such as those employed in public service. These people are likely to reject consumerism and to spend their leisure time and energy on intellectual pursuits such as music or rambling.
- **Undistinctive** – these are the traditional middle classes who belong to clubs and organisations such as the National Trust or golf and leisure clubs. They are likely to form part of middle management in organisations.

THE WORKING CLASSES

Any analysis of the working class must begin with the central problem of Marxism. Despite the seeming accuracy of so many of Marx's analyses of social relationships, his predictions of the development of society have been inaccurate. Marx believed that the Socialist Revolution would occur within or just after the end of his lifetime. This has clearly not happened, neither has the polarisation of social classes into two distinct groups occurred. This central anomaly of Marxism has provoked an enormous amount of research interest since his death.

Marx saw the working class as an oppressed mass of people at the base of society. He believed that the working class would develop a political consciousness where they would work together for each other (collectivism) and he predicted the expansion of the working classes through the process of proletarianisation.

- **Proletarianisation of work** – work becomes deskilled. Workers become reduced to minding machines that do the work previously accomplished by skilled workers.
- **Proletarianisation of society** – society itself becomes urbanised and poor.
- **Political proletarianisation** – the proletariat will begin to work together and develop a class-consciousness.

EMBOURGEOISEMENT THESIS

After the Second World War had ended, western societies enjoyed a period of prosperity which arose from rebuilding and which was particularly evident in the USA which had escaped the worst ravages of the impact of war on its own territory. Compared to all previous societies, people were living longer, eating better, were well educated and could enjoy the benefits of technological development in their homes and their lives. The optimism of the time gave rise to the widely held theory that the working classes were losing their separate identity and becoming more like the middle classes in values, behaviour and expectations. The economist Galbraith is associated with the view that the working class were losing their separate identity as a prelude to a new classless society.

AFFLUENT WORKERS?

A highly detailed research project designed to test the embourgeoisement thesis by **Goldthorpe, Lockwood, Bechofer and Platt** (1968) resulted in three books based around the lives of car workers in Luton. At a surface level, these workers fitted the pattern described by the embourgeoisement thesis. They were comparatively well paid and could earn more from overtime. Many were homeowners and they spent their money on the newly available consumer goods such as televisions and washing machines that were arriving on the market priced for mass sale.

Deeper analysis through questionnaire and interview revealed that their lives were qualitatively different from those of middle management. They worked longer hours, but were alienated from their work, viewing it instrumentally. Their social and home lives were organised differently from those of their middle class colleagues, being more home centred and privatised. They may have moved away from the lives of the traditional working class but embourgeoisement was not taking place. Goldthorpe et al argued that a new form of working class was developing as an adaptation of old patterns.

This work was updated by **Devine** (1992), using a smaller sample. Many of her findings were similar to those of the original affluent worker studies. However, her sample was working in a different economic climate from the group described by Goldthorpe et al. Redundancy and unemployment were a real concern for these families. Other changes had taken place in that their wives were also in the employment market. Their lifestyles were not middle class, but neither did they fit the patterns of the traditional working class.

CREWE AND PARTISAN DEALIGNMENT THESIS

Crewe (1992) attempts to account for the breakdown of the traditional link between working class voting and the Labour Party, a theory known as partisan dealignment. He too subscribes to the thesis that a 'new working class' is emerging.

Table 12:	
OLD WORKING CLASS	NEW WORKING CLASS
Live in traditional working-class communities centred on traditional industry and coalfields	Live in the southern part of the country because of availability of work
Belong to unions and have strong sense of loyalty	Belong to unions for self-protection
Work in old nationalised industries	Work in private concerns for large factories
Live in council or ex-council housing	Have invested in their own homes

DAHRENDORF AND THE DISINTEGRATION OF THE WORKING CLASS

Dahrendorf (1992), in contrast, argues the case for a fragmented working class that has arisen from the different varieties of work available. He divides the working class into three distinct layers, which are not dissimilar from those identified by the Registrar General's 1911 Index of Social Class. Taking his stance from Weber and pluralism, he sees three distinct groupings: skilled, semi-skilled and unskilled working class. He sees the importance of unions as not uniting, but dividing the working class as they attempt to maintain pay differentials between different status and skill groups within organisations.

PAHL AND THE DECOMPOSITION THESIS

Pahl (1984) worked with working-class households in Kent. He too suggested that the working class was itself becoming more divided and that the division was between those in regular work and those who were unemployed or drifting in and out of casual labour. He suggested that it was in the areas where people were mostly employed in declining primary and manufacturing industries that traditional working class people were able to hold on to their values. These people were those who were most likely to form part of a new and growing underclass. He also distinguished a 'new' working class who had secure jobs in assembly work and light industry and who adopted middle-class habits such as home ownership and who enjoyed a comfortable lifestyle.

THE UNDERCLASS THESIS

WHO MAKES UP THE UNDERCLASS?

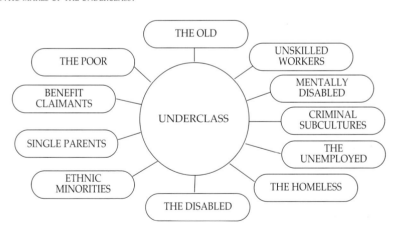

NOTE THAT MANY PEOPLE MAY FALL INTO MORE THAN ONE OF THESE CATEGORIES

This is arguably one of the most significant debates currently taking place within the study of social stratification and differentiation. The term is used widely in the media and in sociology but there is very little agreement as to who comprises the underclass or what characteristics members of the underclass share. The concept of an underclass of poor and deprived people is not a new one – it roughly equates to Marx's reserve pool of labour (lumpenproletariat) and Marx himself was critical of the group, seeing in them the worst characteristics of humanity.

In the early 1970s, the term was used sympathetically by Giddens (1973) to describe those whom society had passed over and who faced massive deprivation and social inequality with working conditions below even those of the working class. At the same time, other social commentators were using the term negatively to describe a class of people who have little self-sufficiency but rely on social security benefits to survive. The term 'dole scrounger' was widely used in the press to describe those who lived on benefit. This approach to the analysis of the underclass remains one that complicates any sociological discussion, because writers are split by politics and perspective. The term 'underclass' carries with it connotations and value judgements which make rational debate complex and difficult, but a simplified summary of the main positions is offered in the table below.

Summarised, the main issues to consider are:

- Who comprises the underclass? (a sociological and a media debate)
- How large is the underclass? (a sociological and a policy debate)
- How can the problem of the underclass be solved? (a social policy debate)
- Do the underclass constitute a separate social group within or beneath the working class? (a purely sociological debate and therefore obviously a prime target for questioning under examination conditions).

	Table 13:	
	RIGHTWING	LEFTWING
Perspective	Cultural view	Structural view
Who are the underclass?	Welfare claimants who have developed a culture of crime and dependency. The lazy and morally degenerate.	The poor and deprived who have little access to the increased wealth of society.
Origins of the underclass	The welfare state. The attitudes and culture of the poor create the problems they experience.	The structure of society. The attitudes and the culture of the poor may have some relevance to their situation.
How large is the underclass?	Large and growing due to the policies of welfare dependency which encourage poor moral values. This group is a threat to the norms of society.	Growing due to changes in the nature of employment which makes the underclass of less value in the workplace due to their lack of skills.
Solving the problems of	Changes in the welfare structure which encourage	Changes in the welfare structure which target the

the underclass	people to work. Education in moral standards and the responsibilities of citizenship.	very poor and the weakest, so that others must seek work. Education in the skills needed for work.
Writers associated with these or similar views	Jordan Murray Saunders	Giddens Field Dahrendorf

THE UNDERCLASS AND THE NEW RIGHT

Murray (1996), an American commentator visited Britain in the early 1990s and was widely reported for his views that the underclass formed a 'disease' in society. The poor were to blame for their own poverty because they had become dependent on benefits and were self-destructive in their habits. *The Sunday Times* had sponsored Murray in his research and his ideas were therefore widely reported in the print based media of the time and gained much credence. Politicians supported his ideas about the underclass in the then Conservative and New Right government. Saunders and other writers such as Marsland who contributed to right Wing think tanks also attempted to identify the characteristics of the underclass. Four main characteristics were identified:

- **Multiple deprivation** – (poverty is multi-factorial – single parenthood, ethnic minority and unemployment)
- **Marginalisation** – (located in sink estates, do not contribute to society)
- **Dependency** – (rely on state to take on responsibilities of parents or husbands towards their children and to give money)
- **Fatalistic** – (see everything as someone else's problem and not their own, do not attempt to alter their situation).

LEFTWING AND NEW LABOUR VIEWS OF THE UNDERCLASS

The leftwing and Marxist derived views of the underclass are by no means as unanimous as the New Right views. Dahrendorf, for instance, considers that the underclass have developed a culture which is dependent and fatalistic, but places the blame on the economic circumstances in which they find themselves. Brown and Madge (1982) found no evidence of a transmitted culture of poverty because families and individuals seemed to be able to move in and out of poverty and few children of the poor were themselves poor.

RECONCILING MARXISM AND WEBERIANISM

Throughout the 1970s and 1980s there were attempts to introduce realism into sociology. Many influential writers and thinkers have tried to reconcile and draw on the best of all of the great meta-narratives such as Marxism, functionalism and interactionalism into 'New' theorising. There has also been a similar trend in the study of stratification and it is these theories that will be studied in the following section.

RUNCIMAN AND ECONOMIC ROLES

Runciman (1990) has taken notions of class structure from Marxism but also draws on Weber to look at the market situation of workers. He sees class as being a function of economic role and the amount of power that it gives to an individual in the class structure. He divides his notion of economic power into a three-part system which reflects Weber's tendency to sub-divide into threes:

- *Marketability* – the ability to sell one's skill or ability in the employment market.
- *Control* – the right to manage either material or labour assets
- *Ownership* – the ownership of the means of production.

He has created a seven class model of British society using the three-part system as the basis for his theorising:

1 **Upper class** – owners of the means of production or those with exceptional marketability for their skills
2 **Upper middle class** – higher-grade professionals, senior civil servants and those on high salaries
3 **Middle middle class** – lower professionals, middle managers and small owners of businesses
4 **Lower middle class** – white-collar workers
5 **Skilled working class** – carpenters and builders
6 **Unskilled working class** – shop assistants and factory workers
7 **Underclass** – benefit claimants, long-term unemployed and the unfit for work.

Although the model is useful in that it introduces the concept of the underclass into the analysis, practically, it varies little from many of those already created by previous writers in the field such as Goldthorpe and Lockwood which show a tendency to sub-divide the middle classes endlessly and yet ignore social and status divisions within the working classes.

GIDDENS AND STRUCTURATION THESIS

Giddens's (1984) structuration thesis is part of a much wider analysis of the geo-politics that is related to the **globalisation** thesis. Globalisation suggests that the world is becoming a smaller place and that individual cultures are tending to be subsumed into a global mass culture. He considers instead the nation state as operating in four different spheres:

1   The industrial economy
2   The financial system
3   Politics
4   The military.

Structuration, for Giddens, refers to the way that people and their society both affect each other. Giddens redefines the term 'social structure' as an individualistic concept and argued that people have choices within their social structure and exercise those choices. Giddens's theorising draws on Weberianism and is in direct contrast to Marx who suggests that individuals have no choices, but must act in certain ways in order to survive.

Structuration and traditional sociologies

Structuralism
Society (structure) affects people and creates individuals

Interpretivism
People (agency) create and maintain concepts of reality

Structuration thesis
People (agency) create society (structure) which then affects and creates people (agency) who then go on to affect the way that society works (structure) which then affects the way that people behave which then …

POSTMODERNISM AND THE END OF CLASS

Postmodernism has been used as a term to refer to the social changes different societies have experienced over the last thirty years. It has been suggested that we live in a post-modern world where class no longer has any significance. People no longer share a common class culture. Being middle class, for example, can mean very different things to different people. It can be represented by a house in the suburbs and annual holidays abroad, or perhaps the ability to purchase designer clothes, partake in weekly recreational activities and have access to global communication via a home PC. Therefore postmodernists argue that there is a growing divide between the lifestyles of social groups.

Social class is seen by postmodernists to be becoming increasingly divorced from culture. Lash and Urry (1987) argue that increasing globalisation through media saturation has had the effect of separating individuals from any traditionally held identities. People no longer feel any affiliation to their class background, but instead soak up the images of different cultures around the world that are offered continuously through media advertising, news and entertainment. Consequently, if the postmodernists are correct, the notion of social class in Britain will soon end in **fragmentation**, with classes constantly swinging between unstable identities. Stratification and differentiation will remain, because capitalism is based on inequality, but any cultural association with others in a similar socio-economic position will cease to occur because we can 'pick and mix' identities from a global 'sweet jar' called the mass media.

Summary and Conclusion

Social class has been central to a sociological understanding of social inequality, only recently being supplemented by notions of gender, ethnicity and age as additional determinants of disadvantage. However, the concept of class has, since the 1980s, been challenged for relying too heavily on occupational status for the formation of class as identity and reason for social action. Traditional theorists have identified individual class groupings and used these as the basis for explaining common characteristics in lifestyles and social experience. Postmodernists, however, have stated that there no longer exist any unified class culture and social class, and even the social inequalities to which they refer, no longer exist.

Sociological Terminology exercise

Look at the following terms and be sure that you understand their meaning. Use them in your examination work:

> Managerial revolution; Aristocracy; Old boys network; Bourgeoisie; Manual and non manual work; Proletarianisation; Embourgeoisement thesis; Fragmentation; Superclass; Underclass.

Group work

Each individual should make a report on any original piece of sociological research that relates to the study of social class in Britain. Use the actual book, or refer to a variety of textbooks that report the work.

Write a report of less than 750 words and make a short presentation of approximately five minutes or less presenting your report to the class. You will ensure that you have enough copies of your report for the rest of the class to each have their own version of your work.

Structure of the report

- **Source** – use Harvard referencing to give the name, date, title and publisher.
- **Objective** – what was the purpose of the research? Explain something of the theory and the background to the research.
- **Methodology** – what did the researcher/s do? Describe the methods used and then offer an explanation of why the researcher chose the methodology that s/he did.
- **Findings** – what were the results of the research? Offer three or four key findings.
- **Evaluation** – what do you actually think of the research? Suggest criticisms of it and point out its strengths.

Coursework

1 You may wish to approach people in your local area who could reasonably be considered to be upper class, either as landowners or as owners of wealth and industry. Your work would have to be qualitative because you will not be allowed to approach anything like a significant number of wealthy people to attempt a numerical study!

You may find that many people of this social background will be willing to cooperate with your study as long as you are not confrontational in any respect.

Ask about how they acquired their wealth and position, ask about what it means to them. You could ask lifestyle questions such as where they were educated or their careers to date. Avoid asking questions about how they spend their money or anything that would be too personal. Some people from this social class have a strong tradition of duty and service to the community; think, for instance, of the attitudes of the Royal Family towards charities and community groups.

Send an outline of your questions in advance, and even if people are not willing to be surveyed in person, then they may send you back some written answers to add to your work. Remember, letters of rejection can also be illuminating documents!

2 It is simple to find a sample of people who could reasonably be considered working class. Most of us fit into this category. Be warned; if you are not of it yourself, there is a very real danger of seeming to be patronising or even

to give the impression of examining people as specimens if you study people from a background not your own. Because there is this danger, then it would make considerable sense to create a numerical study in which quantitative data is more significant than qualitative data.

Ask questions about lifestyle choices such as spending patterns or holiday choices. Do working and middle-class people really have different patterns of consumption and lifestyle? Is it possible that middle class sociologists even try to exaggerate the differences for reasons of snobbery?

Revision hints

Postmodernism has not been a popular topic with examination boards yet, but when this type of theorising becomes more popular and widely known then students can expect to see a variety of questions appearing which test this particular understanding. The question of the significance of social class is not just a sociological position; politicians such as Tony Blair and John Major have been equally at pains to suggest that class is not important in modern Britain. As a result, theories of fragmentation should be at the forefront of your thinking. Is class still important in our culture? Are we still the products of our social class backgrounds in the way that people once were?

Practice Questions

Evaluate the evidence to suggest that there is a significant underclass in British society.

Evaluate the evidence to suggest that social class can affect a person's lifestyle in contemporary Britain.

This is a classic synoptic question in that you will need to draw on a wide range of sociological knowledge and understandings. In the introduction paragraph, you will need to define your terms. Consider, what is social class? Explain in two or three sentences the difficulties attendant on defining class. You will need to refer to theoretical accounts of social class. You will also need to explain the meaning of the term 'lifestyle' or 'life chances' with reference to postmodernism. A very good candidate may consider questioning the terms on which the discussion is to be based.

The body of the essay requires a full explanation of how social class can affect life style in modern Britain. You will need to develop a range of understandings drawn from all areas of the course that you have studied. A few suggestions for answers are offered below, but you should draw the evidence from your own understanding of the issues and your own personal study.

- Your theoretical discussion should concentrate on the class consciousness versus fragmentation debates. There is a serious question to answer as to whether class dictates lifestyle or life chance and consumer choice is the only significant element in people's lives.

- How can social class affect your earning potential in a job? Prove that, as a general rule, people in higher social classes tend to earn more than people in lower social classes. Use evidence from any source to support this idea. Use some of the following ideas: qualifications, education, pay rates, training, status and prestige.

- Social class can affect your health. Prove that, as a general rule, people in lower social classes are less healthy than people in higher social classes. Use some of the following ideas: diet, quality of housing, working conditions and education.

- Social class can affect your educational attainment. Prove that, as a general rule, people from wealthier homes have a better chance of educational success than people from poorer homes. Use some of the following ideas. Mention attitudes, motivation, quality of schools, ability to pay for equipment, 'knowing the system'.

- Conclusion: How important is social class in affecting people's lives? Give a simple answer summarising the points in the previous paragraphs. Remember that you should refer to studies, to research evidence and theoretical understandings throughout this essay.

5

SOCIAL MOBILITY

THIS CHAPTER IS concerned with the examination of the extent to which Britain can be described as an open society, a society that enables movement between strata. There are a number of strands to this debate. Can individuals change their position in the stratification system within the space of their own lives or over generations? Equally interesting is the question of whether whole social groups have risen or descended within the status and class systems that operate in contemporary society.

Many societies operate **closed systems** of stratification, thereby disabling any social mobility. The pre 1945 caste system of the Indian subcontinent and the colour bar system of apartheid South Africa provide excellent examples of closed systems. People in those cultures were born into a social position and remained in those status groups until death; they married within their groups and their children were condemned to live within the conventions that applied to their social positions. In Britain, however, it has been argued that a high status position can afford some protection for the less able children of the wealthy from descent in the social strata. Therefore social closure within our society may be more prevalent than it first appears.

Table 14: *Theories, concepts and issues in this chapter*		
WRITERS	CONCEPTS AND CONCERNS	KEY ISSUES
Glass (1954)	The relative openness of British society	British society is open but there is elite self-recruitment
Oxford Mobility Study (1980)	To replicate and test Glass	There is long-term mobility

Halsey (1980)	The relationship between education and mobility	There is limited relationship between education and mobility. It offers opportunity for some but restricts others.
Heath (1981)	Uses Goldthorpe's data to test mobility.	Women tend to be focussed into certain areas in the occupational structure
Essex Mobility Study (1988)	To test openness of British society and to include women in data	Upward mobility is possible and education plays a part in this.
Bottomore (1966)	Elites	The closure of an elite is a barrier to democracy
Saunders (1990)	New Right causes of social inequality	Social inequality is desirable and may reflect character and ability of individuals
Lockwood (1979)	Proletarianisation thesis	The class position of the clerk has fallen
Wright Mills (1956)	Proletarianisation thesis	The middle classes are deskilled and losing status

OPEN AND CLOSED SOCIETIES

Societies vary according to the ability of individuals or social groups to change their position in the stratification system; this movement between strata is known as social mobility.

- Closed societies are characterised by a rigid structure in which a person is born into a status group and will inevitably die within that status group. Individuals cannot change their social positioning whatever their abilities or the circumstances of their life. There is no chance of social mobility. The term used to describe a social position determined by birth is 'ascribed status'. Examples include pre-separation India where the caste system dominated society.
- Open societies are characterised by a system where movement between strata is both possible and accepted. Often it is claimed that such a society is meritocratic in that social status may be determined by ability and determination. The USA is often considered to be an open society; the myth of the American Dream offers the possibility that any citizen can make it 'from log cabin (ie conditions of poverty) to the White House'. Very few people seriously believe that Britain is a truly open society, so the question becomes one of assessing the extent to which it is possible for people to change their class position through social mobility.

SOCIAL MOBILITY

Commentators in Britain generally identify two forms of social mobility: vertical and horizontal.

- **Vertical social mobility** describes movement between strata both up and down the stratification system. It can usually be seen as an example of **long-range** mobility, displaying a change in class status and can be examined through:
- **Inter-generational mobility** which describes movements in social class **between** generations, so that the children of a lower paid worker may achieve high status jobs, or vice versa.
- **Intra-generational mobility** which would be used to describe social mobility **within** one lifetime, such as when an individual begins his or her career in one status occupation, but who moves up or down through the class system within the span of a working life.
- **Horizontal mobility** which is also known as lateral mobility. This is a geographical term used to describe movement around the country to new forms of similar employment. This can be seen as **short-range** mobility, because there is little change in the individual's class status.

Activity
Create a detailed family tree for your family with each person marked by their first job and their current job, or the occupation from which they retired. If you can, you might also offer a rough indication of the year in which each person was born. How much evidence of mobility within your own family are you able to discover? Is the mobility upward or downward, is it inter-generational or intra-generational? Pool the maps for the whole class in a wall display. What do you learn about the patterns of mobility within your local area over the last one hundred years from this exercise?

RELATIVE AND ABSOLUTE SOCIAL MOBILITY

Social mobility can also be categorised as relative or absolute to show the type of mobility that is occurring:

- Relative social mobility – this is the chance different classes have of achieving social mobility. For example, if working class and middle class workers both went after the same middle class jobs, the relative chances of the working class workers getting those jobs are much less than the middle class workers. Therefore relative mobility enables researchers to assess the relative openness of Britain.

- Absolute social mobility – this refers to the total amount of social mobility in society. For example, if a particular class has experienced a lot of social mobility, whether up or down, this will produce a high rate of absolute mobility.

OPERATIONALISING SOCIAL MOBILITY

There are a number of practical problems when conducting research into whether social mobility is possible and has taken place within the class structure of Britain.

- Samples of the population need to be quite large in order to represent the whole of Britain.
- Class itself is not a universally agreed social category
- It might be that mobility has been easier for certain generations, even since the Second World War than for others depending upon the availability of certain types of work or the conditions of the economy.
- Women have not been represented in much of the work done on social mobility despite their presence in the workforce in small numbers in the earlier parts of this century to their present very strong position in the labour market now.
- This form of research tends to be quantitative and ignores the impact of social mobility upon individuals and family. Note however, that Bertaux and Thompson (1997) have recently argued for a qualitative approach and the use of family histories in gaining an understanding of mobility.
- Definitions of social mobility vary. It could be seen in terms of income or it could be defined in terms of status. There is no consensus on this point among sociologists, which makes comparisons of data collected on social mobility very problematic.

THE HISTORY OF RESEARCH INTO SOCIAL MOBILITY

The earliest studies into social mobility and the class structure depended upon statistical analysis and some of these projects, in the days before computer analysis, were quite remarkable undertakings. They reflect the significance of research into social stratification for social planners and commentators at the time when these large-scale projects were undertaken. Data collected on social mobility was used to determine many factors affecting social classes in Britain, such as size, formation, life chances and responses to mobility.

GLASS AND 'SOCIAL MOBILITY IN BRITAIN' (1954)

Glass (1954) conducted a large-scale empirically based survey on social class in 1949. He studied the inter-generational mobility of men only, in England and Wales. He drew a number of conclusions from his study which include:

- While individuals do in fact move up or down the system, it is generally short range and within categories so that few people break through from manual work to professional work.
- There was inter-generational mobility with many sons taking higher status occupations than their fathers, while others descended through the stratification system.
- Generally however, the pattern was one of sons taking jobs with a similar status to those of their fathers.
- The middle classes are filled with the children of the middle classes that implies 'elite self recruitment'.
- While it is possible to rise in the system, membership of the middle classes seems to offer children some protection from dropping back through into lower-status work.

Criticisms of this work include the following points:

- The sample included only men.
- The work is now out of date, being nearly fifty years old.
- There was a wide range of middle class and semi-professional social groups in the higher occupational status categories defined but the manual working classes were grouped together and this underplays the significance of status groupings within the working classes at the end of the Second World War.
- There have been arguments as to the accuracy of the sampling procedure and the methodology (Payne, Ford and Robertson, 1977).

THE OXFORD MOBILITY STUDY (1980)

This is also known as the Nuffield Study, because the team that conducted the report were based in Nuffield College, Oxford University. The survey was conducted in 1972, with the sample including males only, aged between 20 and 64 years. The study used a different basis for allocating class position from Glass, one that was based on pay rates and not social standing.

The study was concerned with two elements of mobility:

- Outflow – this is seen as the destination and where people born into a social class complete their careers.
- Inflow – this is the concern with where people in a given social class originate.

Key findings include the following points:

- The study suggested that there was a relatively high incidence of long-range social mobility. This showed movement up through the system, but more limited movement down.
- It suggested an expansion of the middle-class occupations that were being filled by the able children of working-class parents.

- Children of middle class parents were far more likely to achieve middle class jobs than children of working class parents. Therefore the **1:2:4 rule of relative hope** was established, which demonstrated that class position affects your chances of mobility, with middle-class offspring being four times more likely to enter middle-class occupations.

- Interestingly, it made the suggestion that the British middle classes were not a uniform class made up of shared values, because of the diverse class origins of the people who take up middle class occupations.

- The Oxford Mobility data was used by Heath (1981) to suggest that in the elite classes, there is considerable closure, with the products of the public school system maintaining their control over business, commerce and public life.

However much intelligence may be helped or hindered by social environment, there is no doubt that the possession of high intelligence can be of assistance in upward mobility, and that low intelligence is a near fatal bar to it. Obviously this factor applies virtually exclusively to the lower classes. It requires no intelligence at all to be born into the upper classes (although it usually requires, at least, the intelligence to appoint a good accountant to stay there).

O'Donnell (1997:177)

Criticisms of this study include the following points:

- It uses an occupational model of the class structure and this tends to ignore the subjective experience of class.
- It ignores the experience and class position of women.

EDUCATION AND SOCIAL MOBILITY

The data gathered by the Oxford Mobility Study (1980) was applied by Halsey, Heath and Ridge (1980) to consider the relationship between social mobility and education. In their famous study, *Origins and Destinations*, Halsey *et al* suggested that despite professed aims towards meritocracy, the education system had not markedly increased the openness of British society. For some generations of men in the twentieth century, there had been a closure of society and a restriction of opportunity. This pattern was exacerbated by the existence of the public school system that offered the privileged a fast-track route into high-status occupations.

FEMALE MOBILITY

Females are a large and increasing proportion of the workforce. However, many writers on social mobility have ignored them. The assumption that females take their class position from their male relatives distorts social mobility studies for the following reasons:

- Many women are householders in their own right with 21% of families headed by a lone woman.
- Of married women in paid employment, more than half are manual workers in their own right, however, by taking their husband as an indicator of social class only one third are manual workers.
- Studies that overlook half the population are by their very nature invalid and unreliable. The experience of women is just as valid as that of men.

For women, the question of mobility is tied in with their unequal position in the labour market, where they earn considerably less than many males even within the same occupational structure. Heath (1981) suggested that they tend to be concentrated into the lower and middle class positions in society. The Essex mobility study offered the view that patterns of social mobility between men and women are remarkably similar, except that men are more evenly found in all parts of the social system whereas women concentrate in certain occupations.

THE ESSEX MOBILITY STUDY (1988)

Marshall, Rose, Newby and Vogler published their study in 1988, and so their work is more recent than the Oxford Mobility Study. The Essex Mobility Study also collected data on both the inter-generational and intra-generational mobility of women and men in the workforce and can therefore be argued to be more reliable than previous studies. Using Goldthorpe's model of social class, the Essex study produced results which were similar to those of the Oxford study when looking at males, but suggested that females showed a higher rate of absolute mobility, because of their tendency to take on routine office work or to slip into casual low-paid labour. Their findings summarised, suggest that:

- There is upward mobility for many. As the number of middle-class occupations expands, children from the working classes are recruited into professional occupations.
- People from working-class backgrounds have less of a chance of achieving high-status occupations than those from middle-class backgrounds. This shows relative mobility to be similar for both men and women.
- Education plays a significant part in social mobility and for many the education system is a ladder of opportunity.
- Those who do become high achievers tend to take on the attributes of their class of destination and abandon the values and behaviours of their class of origin.

Their figures suggested that males do move through the class system, and that those who originated in working-class families and achieved high-status occupations at some point in their careers were more likely to experience downward mobility in their careers than those who originated in high status families. This suggests that social mobility is a force for conservatism in society.

Points of evaluation of social mobility studies in Britain

- In studying only two generations, it is easy to overlook the history of mobility within families. Jackson and Marsden (1972) in a study of working class boys in grammar school found a pattern which suggested that many of the children had fathers who were working class, but their mothers had originated in middle-class households.
- Studies neglect the unemployed and the underemployed, despite these groups forming a significant part of the class system.
- Many of the studies are not strictly comparable; a whole series of different systems of classifications have been used by writers, with Goldthorpe designing his own.
- Westergaard and Resler (1976) suggest that mobility studies tend to neglect issues of wealth because they concentrate on occupation.
- In relying on a son reporting his father's occupation, unreliability may enter the research as sons either downplay or overplay their parental occupations. It also ignores the influence of mothers; see the point made above by Jackson and Marsden (1972).

Summary of conclusions of mobility studies

- There is a limited degree of mobility for some people into the higher reaches of society.
- The wealthy are able to pass on their social class positions to their children.
- The highest social groups, known as the elite, tend to recruit from within their own ranks, meaning penetration by others is limited.
- There has been an increase in middle class jobs due to an expansion of the service sector of industry since the end of the Second World War.
- There is more upward mobility than downward mobility.

SOCIAL CLOSURE AND THE ELITE

> Democracy, in one of its established meanings, implies that there should be a substantial degree of equality among men, both in the sense that all the adult members of a society ought to have, so far as is possible, an equal influence upon those decisions which affect important aspects of the life of the society, and in the sense that inequalities of wealth, of social rank, or of education and access to knowledge, should not be so considerable as to result in the permanent subordination of some groups of men to others in any of the various spheres of social life …
>
> Bottomore (1966:129)

Study point

(i) What are the problems in defining equality?
(ii) Is there evidence that the subordination of one group by another continues in modern Britain?

The term 'elite' implies a form of social superiority above and beyond that implied by a position in the class structure and suggests that those in the upper strata of society are in some way culturally and socially superior to others. The existence of an elite, for Bottomore (1966), was a barrier to democracy and opportunity for all. However, one of the myths that sustain society is the belief that hard work will result in success, success being measured by rising to the top of the social structure. Equality of opportunity is seen to support the most able in their rise to the top of the stratification system. New Right sociologists, such as Saunders (1990), argue that social inequality as a reflection of equal opportunity to fail or succeed is desirable and could even be a reflection of genetic or biological differences. Woodhams (1995) points out that this belief tacitly accepts and underpins notions that inequality is 'natural' and good for society.

Parkin (1979) offers the suggestion that the existence of a degree of social mobility is necessary in a capitalist society because it can act as a mechanism for social cohesion. The able people rise through the system, abandoning their class loyalties and becoming absorbed into the value structures of the class that they join. Revolutionary potential among the workers is defused, as the potential leaders of the working class become the leaders of capitalist society.

PROLETARIANISATION THESIS

Proletarianisation thesis is the name given to the idea that groups within the middle classes will become absorbed into the working classes as capitalism develops. In essence this is a concern of Marxists, or those who wish to test or refute Marx, because the issue is one of the development (or lack) of class-consciousness. The terminology of the debate illustrates this point. There are two basic forms of this thesis:

- *Proletarianisation of action* – the middle classes behave as members of the working class in terms of voting allegiance or through joining in working-class political activity such as trade unionism.
- *Proletarianisation of condition* – the middle classes lose market or income status so that their work is less autonomous and professional in terms of relationships with employers or in terms of pay and conditions than it once was.

LOCKWOOD AND THE 'BLACKCOATED WORKER'

One of the most important studies of social class, which looked at the social mobility of whole groups of workers rather than focussing on the relative social mobility of individuals within the workforce, was Lockwood's (1989) classic study of the 'blackcoated worker'. Lockwood considered the case of the clerk. Historically, to be a clerk was to be lower middle class and in a relatively high status profession. Clerks were white collared workers who had good working conditions and high wages in comparison with skilled manual workers. They were often well educated. Lockwood noted however, that by the 1950s when his study was being conducted, there were two separate changes affecting the class position of clerks.

- Clerical workers were becoming proletarianised.
- The professional classes were growing in size and numbers.

The wage position of the clerk has consistently declined and in some cases unskilled manual work was better paid than clerical work. This was considered evidence of proletarianisation. A number of points need to be made however:

- Clerical work has become feminised so that whereas clerical work once was the privilege of men, it is now female work.
- Technology has taken from the skills of the clerk, who needed to have good handwriting and arithmetic. Machines can, however, do this work.
- Clerical workers enjoy pleasant working conditions and often have fringe benefits that are not immediately apparent.
- Many clerical workers can be promoted through the system, although it is generally the qualified who are now fast-tracked in this way.
- Lockwood claims that clerical workers see themselves as having middle class status. Indeed this may be true, if clerical work is feminised, women are considered to take their class status from males.

WRIGHT MILLS AND THE 'WHITE COLLAR'

Wright Mills (1956) undertook research into the American middle classes to test proletarianisation in his famous study of white collared workers. He argued that there had been a loss of status for clerical workers and that they had therefore become conspicuous consumers to maintain their social differences from the working classes. He argued that insecurity had led them to experience 'status panic' and that they had resorted to joining trade unions in order to safeguard their lessening incomes. Consequently, white-collar workers may have been proletarianised in their occupations, but in their lifestyles and attitudes they remained middle class.

In terms of evaluating proletarianisation thesis, consider the following points:

- While incomes between the middle classes and the skilled working classes seem to have converged slightly, the attitudes, behaviours and values of these two social groups remain different.
- The majority of white-collar and clerical workers seem to see themselves as middle class and do not identify with the working classes.
- There has been some evidence to suggest that social class is less significant in people's behaviours and lifestyles than it was in the earlier parts of this century.

HOW OPEN IS BRITISH SOCIETY?

Any consideration of the possibility for social mobility within Britain must be done within the context of the widening gap between rich and poor. Survey after survey comes to the inescapable conclusion that inequality is growing in Britain. Whole social groups are relatively less well off or better off than they were in the past. To what extent can the talented individuals break through from poverty or the less talented among the well off descend through the system? Using evidence from the Oxford Mobility Study, Heath (1981) suggested that mobility upwards through the system is achievable and that many men from working class backgrounds do cross into middle class work and rise through the social strata into higher grade work. He further suggested that the middle classes use technical and vocational qualifications as a route for their less academic children into skilled manual work which offers better opportunities for financial success than low-skilled clerical work. However, his work is now over twenty years old and the intervening years of Conservative rule (1979–96) based on the individualistic principles of the New Right, have left our society as one which experiences high unemployment, insecurity of employment and a tax system which is non-redistributive.

Much recent work in this field is actually based on economic analyses of social inequality rather than on sociological debate. The arguments centre on an underlying set of concerns with the impact of low employment, contraction of the labour market and the extent to which an underclass is developing as a result of social policy. A typical example of such work would be an unpublished thesis that can be located via the Sosig website. Ramos (1999) argued that Britain is a closed society in which inequality is endemic. He bases his arguments on statistics provided by the British Household Panel Survey and analyses the monthly earnings of male full-time employees using the British Household Panel Study for the period 1991–95. He claims that individual earnings differentials tend to be lifelong in character, although the galloping shift towards increased social inequality typical of the Conservative government is slowing. Low earners will in probability remain low earners all through their lives and this particular tendency is increased for the older and younger members of the employment sector.

However, the evidence is not absolutely clear cut and other writers such as Savage (1995), who bases his arguments on work by Goldthorpe (1980), suggest that movement between the social classes is frequent and both upwards and downwards through the class structure. Savage argues that social mobility is leading to a fragmentation of social values and culture among the middle classes. This is a post-modernist stance, but draws from Weberian and Marxist positions in that it notes a state of society where conflict and differentiation is the norm; however, it sees this as taking place *within* classes rather than *between* them.

Summary and Conclusion

The main issue within this chapter is to consider not only whether Britain is an open society where movement between social classes is possible, but also that it actually happens in such significant quantities that it affects the nature of the class system itself. If social mobility does occur, is it only the expansion of the middle classes absorbing the talented working classes, or are people downwardly socially mobile too? Does wealth and status protect the children of the middle classes from descending into poverty and deprivation or do the offspring of the disadvantaged have opportunities for success? Certainly at times in this century the middle classes have opened up to allow mass movement up through the system; this was aided by the expansion of higher education in the 1960s and 1970s and the decline of the manufacturing industries coupled with the rise of the service industries. However, it is arguable whether the same opportunities exist today for the gifted members of the working class. The debate tends to focus on the issue of whether people can move up or down in the system and to neglect issues of the comparative stability of the class system as a whole, so that inequities of access to wealth and power remain sidelined in discussion.

We have seen twenty years of widening inequality in our society. Indeed, the proletarianisation thesis seems to imply that the expansion of the middle classes and the advent of technologies has in fact reduced the status and power of the middle classes so that there is very little difference between the skilled manual worker and the low paid professional worker. The picture that emerges of British society from mobility studies is that the top layers of society seem to be remarkably stable and that they are closed to penetration from below, and that the lowest classes too are a cohesive unit with the children of the poor growing to be poor themselves. The bulk of the debate centres on the central layers of the system that are generally fluid in structure. You might like to consider that the class structure is similar to a custard slice. There is a relatively stable top and bottom but the centre is thickly viscous. It is this fluid layer that motivates the debate and gives rise to speculation as to the nature of the society in which we live.

STUDY GUIDE

Sociological Terminology exercise

Look at the following terms and be sure that you understand their meaning. Use them in your examination work:

Social mobility; Inter-generational mobility; Intra-generational mobility; Open societies; Closed societies; Absolute mobility; Relative mobility; Class solidarity; Class identity.

Group work

Create a wall display of people who have achieved social success in our society. How many came from relatively poor backgrounds? What is the best route for poorer people to achieve social success in your view?

Coursework

As a study of social class and aspirations take a wide sample of students from a school or a college. Design a simple questionnaire asking students for information about their parental occupations, what jobs their parents would like them to have and what type of work they would like to undertake. Is there a link between their occupational aspiration and their current position in the class structure?

Revision hints

Ensuring that you can list the main research projects best covers this topic. List the evidence that supports the view that social mobility is possible in Britain today; this is a relevant point if one of your substantive topics in the examination is education because you may be required to consider whether education does provide a ladder of opportunity for people. Look at questions of the increasing inequality of British society and consider whether social mobility is an illusion, with the middle classes recruiting from the poorer classes in times of expanding opportunity and then closing ranks again when the available high-status work can be filled by their own children.

Exam hints

- *What does the study of social mobility tell us about the significance of class in British society?*
- *Evaluate the evidence to support the view that Britain is an 'open' society.*

There is a great deal of evidence to support the view that Britain is an open society because many of the class barriers that were once endemic to British society are clearly breaking down: regional accents are socially acceptable and individuals from relatively poor backgrounds do seem to become rich and famous through the exercise of talent or some other marketable quality. However, do the numbers of people who do break through into the ranks of the rich and famous really represent a significant social trend? This is the point at which you will need to refer to the statistical evidence and this shows a very different reality, one where those from poorer backgrounds seem condemned to reproduce the patterns of their parents. The question of the relative openness or closure of society also provides a significant test of Marxism, because Marx described a society which would polarise into two opposing groups.

6

GENDER INEQUALITY

THIS CHAPTER IS concerned with the ascribed status that is associated with gender. Gender refers to socially constructed forms of behaviour that are expected by society in association with each sex, for example women are feminine and men are masculine. In our society, gender is a remarkably significant determinant of life chance and lifestyle with women still earning significantly less than males and being far more likely to live and to end their lives in poverty. The rule of males and control of society is known as **patriarchy** and it is this that feminists seek to address in a variety of ways. Many radical feminists claim that society is misogynistic; they claim men hate and fear women and this too should be considered. However, gender does not merely affect the life chances of women and it is facile to see gender as being a 'female problem'. Males too are under pressure to conform to gender stereotypes and it is argued that these stereotypes can be destructive resulting in boys becoming the new underachievers in education and in the employment market. Although gender is a form of differentiation in our society, is it more significant than divisions imposed by class? Do middle- and working-class women share the same concerns? Do middle class women have more in common with middle class men than other women from ethnic minorities or from the working class? Do black and white women share experiences in common? Postmodernists have added to the debate by suggesting that gender is now an optional behaviour, whereas once it was an established pattern of behaviour. People are now freer to adopt gendered behaviours in a way that suits their personal needs. Gender is therefore only one of a number of factors that influence the social possibilities for any one person.

Table 15: *Theories, concepts and issues in this chapter*		
WRITERS	CONCEPTS/CONCERNS	KEY ISSUES
Parsons (1959) Murdock (1949)	Functionalism and the New Right	Are gender roles dictated by biology as well as socialisation?
Engels (1884)	Marxism	patriarchy and the development of private property
Oakley (1974)	Liberal feminism	Legislating for female equality
Barron and Norris (1976) Beechy (1983)	Marxist feminism	The influence of capitalism on gender inequality
Millet (1970) Firestone (1970)	Radical feminism	Are women the victims of men?
Mirza (1997)	Black feminism	The dual effects of race and gender for women
Butler (1993)	Postmodernism	The loss of traditional gender identities
Equal Opportunities Commission	Gender inequality	Has legislation improved the social position of women in Britain?

At the start of the nineteenth century women had little or no legal status and were viewed as the possessions of their menfolk. Certainly the position has changed very quickly in legal and social terms with the main changes taking place since 1945 and the end of the Second World War. Commentators have tied in these changes with the advent of reliable contraception and developments in the nature of work

Table 16: *An overview of some of the reasons for changes in the status of women*	
CHANGE	IMPACT ON LIVES OF WOMEN
Decline in number of children	Women are free free to become part of the work force Female life expectancy has increased.
Increase in educational opportunities	Females are overtaking males in attainment at GCSE Women are part of the professional middle classes
Expansion of social services	Women are free from dependence on men
Legal changes	Women have property rights and right to divorce on same terms as men
Moral changes	Women are freer to have children as single parents The relationship between sexual activity and marriage is looser
Employment changes	Women are less dependent on men for income and this has changed the balance of power in many families
Political activity	Governments are beginning to respond to the fact that females have voting rights and must design legislation that takes into account the needs of women.

FUNCTIONALIST AND ASSOCIATED VIEWS OF GENDER

Functionalist accounts of the position of women in the labour market and the family, such as Parson (1959) and Murdock (1949), are constrained by their need to view all existing social structures as somehow answering the needs of society. This leaves them unable to perceive their views of gender inequality as morally ambiguous; they assume that things are as they are because it is the best possible way for society to function. They view gender roles as being influenced by factors such as biology and suggest that gender roles are learned through socialisation. In other words, women are genetically predisposed to produce and rear offspring, which makes them more suitable for domestic labour, a belief that is reinforced by ascribed gender roles.

Functionalist accounts of gender seem curiously out of date. It is not a position that many sociologists would hold today although it does form part of the conservative theorising of the New Right. It is also popular in America where there has been some considerable reaction to the demands of women for equality of status with males. Scruton (1986) a philosopher of the New Right has argued that it is beneficial for society for men and women to take on differing roles in society because the genders are distinct and do behave and think differently over above cultural conditioning. It is this position that will be challenged by much of the debate in this chapter.

MARXIST ACCOUNTS OF GENDER DIVISION

Marxist accounts of gender tend to begin with analyses of the family and this is a fair reflection of society at the time when women were concerned with the domestic and discouraged from participation in life outside the home. Although the influence of Marxist theorising on the family was not felt until well into this century, Marx's collaborator, Engels published the key text, *The Origin of the Family, Private Property and the State* in 1884. He suggested that patriarchy arose from the development of private property and originated in the need for males to have heirs to pass on their goods to. He needed to be certain that the children his wife produced were in fact, his. Monogamous marriage was a way of controlling female sexuality and restricting freedom so that a male can ensure that the children he rears are his own. There appears to be an element of truth in this analysis, despite the fact that the evidence Engels produced to support the argument was not strong. Many cultures prize virginity in a female and operate under a dual morality with regard to female and male sexuality. To develop the point, note that the moral outcry over young single mothers does not extend to the males who father the children.

People would have been aware of Engels's work, but it did not have a strong impact on the academic literature until the 1960s and 1970s when many female writers began to question the nature of gender relations in our society. Taking Marxist analyses of class as a starting point, and then applying a conflict–structural approach to the study of gender relations produced a startlingly simple set of understandings. The underlying structures of society create inequality and oppression – females need to unite to address questions of patriarchy in the same way that workers need to address questions of capitalism.

FEMINISMS

Feminism and the women's movements have a long and venerable history, but feminism first became influential as a perspective during the 1960s in sociology. However, the term 'feminism' is very misleading because it implies that feminists share a point of view and this is by no means the case. Most commentators agree that there are four main forms of feminism, though more have been identified:

- *Liberal feminism,* which is equated with the battle for equal rights and opportunities.
- *Marxist feminism* which sees capitalism and patriarchy as linked and is concerned with issues of class.
- *Radical feminism* which sees patriarchy as the enemy women should fight, and which argues that the oppression of women by men is more significant than any workplace oppression which may take place.
- *Black feminism* which acknowledges that previous feminist analyses were based on the experiences of white middle class women, necessitating a perspective that concentrated on the social inequality faced by black women caused by racism, sexism and capitalism.

Most forms of feminism share three main points of agreement:

- Males control property and wealth in most societies and so women are denied the power which money can exert over others.
- Males allocate the least pleasant tasks and positions in society to women. They are paid less for undertaking this type of work.
- Men and women are socialised into accepting inequality as being basic to society and somehow normal. They claim that the socialisation process of women trains them to accept an inferior position and that they must challenge this conditioning.

LIBERAL FEMINISM

The social disadvantage experienced by women in Britain resulted in the rise of liberal feminism, which set out to challenge the legal restrictions placed on women. Liberal feminists believe that men and women are equal and that any differentials in their life chances and opportunities in society are manifest from socially constructed gender roles. Therefore they argue that changes in legislation allowing women equal access and opportunity in education and paid employment will reconstruct more equal gender roles.

Oakley (1974) attempted to establish a critique of functionalist assumptions of 'necessary' gender divisions in society. She suggested that the social disadvantage experienced by women in Britain was a consequence of patriarchal social construction, not biology. Her work enabled other liberal feminists to investigate the social influence on prescribed gender behaviour, particularly the influence of legislation. It was no longer accepted that the ability to bear children equated with secondary status within the workplace. Liberal feminists highlighted to the public the subordinated position in the workforce and forced the government into action to address this obvious inequality. In 1970 The Equal Pay Act and in 1975 The Sex Discrimination Act became law and gave women legislated equal rights to men, although the success of this legislation has been strongly debated.

Liberal feminism has been criticised for:

- Not challenging the patriarchy inherent in the legal and social system
- Failing to acknowledge the impact of class and race on the social experiences of women.

MARXIST FEMINISM

The emphasis that Marxism places on economics means that many Marxists and Marxist feminists have looked at the economic position of women in society. There are two ways of looking at this issue:

- The role of women in the workplace and their relationship with capitalism
- The role of women in the home and how it impacts on their position in the workplace.

Women as a reserve army of labour
A large number of theorists are associated with the view that capitalism can draw on women to provide a reserve army of labour, brought in to undercut the wages of males when production is required and put out of work in times of low productivity. An illustration of this theory is the way in which women became part of the labour force during both World Wars but were put out of work again as the soldiers returned home.

Barron and Norris (1976) pointed out that women, are largely excluded from the higher paid, better skilled and most secure jobs in the labour market which they define as being the 'primary labour market'. Instead, they argue that women are concentrated in the 'secondary labour market' of low pay, poor job security and bad working conditions. This they claim is because of a set of social beliefs about the nature of female attitudes to work and their lack of unionisation.

Braverman (1974) in the USA suggested that women are a reserve pool of labour used to supplement the workforce in times of labour shortage. He claims that they enter deskilled work because they will accept lower pay. However, **Carchedi (1987)** an Italian Marxist counters this view when he argues that the feminisation of labour is a significant factor in the proletarianisation of clerical work. If a job becomes feminised, the pay and status of the occupation falls.

Beechy (1983) however, points out that women are not really part of the dual labour market drawn in to merely to replace men, because even when they do work alongside men they are still not paid equally and do not receive promotion. She notes that their lack of union status means that they are easier to employ and to make redundant. **Walby (1986)** however, points out that many trade unions themselves are patriarchal institutions and have a history of rejecting women.

The impact of domestic labour on women

This has been a significant debate because it is clear that the main burden of domestic labour falls on women. Childcare in particular is pointed out as being a problem for women who wish to work.

- **Oakley** (1974) says that all paid work is simply an extension of the type of work that women do in the home: childcare, cleaning and caring.
- **Land** suggests that the inadequacy of childcare facilities in this country limits women's choice of work.
- **Beechey (1983)** claims that although females are able to make small gains in terms of access to work, they are clustered in certain feminised occupations and make up a huge proportion of clerical workers.

Study point
The position of women in the labour market and the difficulties that they have reconciling domestic roles and working roles are very fruitful areas for coursework study. Issues to tackle could be whether females feel that they have experienced discrimination, childcare problems, the nature of female work, the life and employment histories of females in work and the attitudes of different generations and classes to issues of whether women should work or spend time with their young children.

Points of evaluation

Because Marxist feminists link the oppression of women with the rise of capitalism, it cannot fully explain why women were dominated in pre-capitalist and non-capitalist societies (Pilcher, 1993).

RADICAL FEMINISM

Radical accounts of gender suggest that the real cause of female inequality is patriarchy, based on the hatred and fear of desire that men have for women. Much of the significant writing originated in the 1970s and was extremely angry in tone, drawing on Marxism, but emphasising gender as the battleground of social revolution.

Kate Millet and Sexual Politics

Millet (1970) offered an eight point strategy whereby society in general and men in particular were able to dominate and subjugate women. She suggested that the main arguments used against women were as listed, and she then proceeded to refute each in turn:

- **Biological** – male strength is no longer an argument for male domination, as little modern work requires physical strength.
- **Ideological** – males are socialised into a sense of domination and women should attempt to fight this tendency in their sons.
- **Class** – masculinity is a caste status and whatever their social class, all women are seen as inferior to men. Bullying tactics can reinforce this.
- **Education** – educational inequalities force women to take on subordinate roles.
- **Religion** – religion legitimises male dominance so that God is conceived of in masculinist terms
- **Force and laws** – patriarchy is backed up by coercion so that in many cultures violence is used against women as part of their cultural tradition.

As a point of evaluation, you should note that this takes a one-sided view of the debate with females as ever the victims of male oppressors. This may be an oversimplification.

Firestone

Using the terminology of Marxism, Firestone (1970) criticises the Marxist view of gender relations and claims that patriarchy arose through biological imperatives related to the dependency of the child on the mother. She goes on to claim that patriarchy and the need for males to dominate women give rise to capitalism, because they create the need for males to dominate other males. However, this work has been criticised, again for laying victim status on females, and also because child rearing is not always the responsibility of the mother. The child may need primary care for some time, but by three or four, can take on some of its own care.

Study point

The debates around feminism have been among the most controversial and heated within the tradition itself as well as in mainstream sociology. There is a vast and fascinating literature that will repay further study. The Internet has provided a new forum for debate, particularly in the USA, and you are advised to trawl some of the sites to see what you can discover. Gender politics is also linked to sexual and reproductive politics, so many sites will be inaccessible to school computers with filtration systems for sensitive material. Be cautious in your choice of site to visit and do not allow anyone to have your e-mail address or home address.

BLACK FEMINISM

Black feminist thought that rearticulates experiences such as these fosters an enhanced theoretical understanding of how race, gender, and class oppression are part of a single, historically created system.

Hill Collins (1990:230)

Black feminism exists to point out that females have varied life experiences. Previous forms of feminism that do not take account of the life experiences of women who are also black ignore another potent form of inequality in our society – racism. Hill Collins (1990) points out that while white women are disadvantaged by their gender, they are empowered by their race. Black feminists are associated with the attempt to document the experiences of ethnic minority women within education, the workforce and in families. One of the most significant names associated with this type of research work in Britain is Safia-Mirza (1997) who is noted for pointing out that Afro-Caribbean girls in school often exceed their teachers' expectations of them as an act of resistance against the negative attitudes which they experience in education. A recurrent theme in her work is that of countering the negative stereotyping endemic to our society and pointing out achievements that women have had in fighting both racism and sexism in our culture.

FEMINISM AND THE BACKLASH

Recent work by the feminist Faludi (1992) has pointed to an interesting change of attitude in public life that attacks women. Although it is claimed that women have achieved equality, they are constantly being told that they are miserable by the media. The villains of films and dramas such as **Basic Instinct** are career women and they are portrayed in an increasing negative way; they may have careers but they are still shown as dissatisfied and unhappy. Faludi offers an optimistic view of patterns of female incursion into working rather than domestic life. She claims that married domestic women experience significant psychological and physical stress symptoms. The picture presented in the media is merely an ideological attempt by males to turn back the clock and reclaim power. Interestingly, her most recent work has been concerned with how males construct their sense of their masculine identity. The criticism of feminism does not come solely from men and the media; Paglia (1994) has become prominent in recent years for expressing heavy criticism of the aims of feminism, despite claiming to be a feminist herself. She has become something of a hate figure in many circles for suggesting that women have become the winners in today's society by using their victim status as a weapon for individual success.

Activity
Attempt a content analysis of many modern American television dramas such as *Ally McBeal* or *Sex and the City* that have professional women as their central characters. What ideology of the role of women is on offer?

POSTMODERN ACCOUNTS OF GENDER

Postmodernism has entered the feminist debate, offering an interpretation of female oppression that is based on differentiation. Postmodern feminism suggests that all women have very different social experiences; therefore there can never be a generalised explanation of their subordination in modern industrial society (Jardine, 1985). Women now participate in society in an uncertain role, based on media representations of gender identity that sway between the empowered, liberated woman and the traditional image of mother–housewife.

Postmodernism, as a theory apart from feminism, does not examine issues of gender inequality, suggesting instead that gender is not oppositional. Men and women are not seen to be in formal battles for power, but instead are on a continuum of gendered behaviours. Postmodernists are more interested in those who experience gender misalignment, such as transsexuals, or who are homosexual.

It is not only ideas about gender – about the differences or non-differences between males and females – that are changing in the general onslaught against the modern concept of identity. People are also (as you may have noticed) challenging traditional ideas about sexual behaviour and about the meanings we attribute to it.

Simon (1996:152)

There is a growing body of debate within the postmodern perspective that examines how individuals create their own sense of their gendered identity and this is reflected in the fact that many of the better bookshops now have a section on Gay Studies. One of the best known writers in this more recent tradition is Butler (1993) of the University of California, who is also associated with Queer Theory. She claims that different gender behaviours are appropriate and used for different situations. As a point of evaluation, this may well be true of California and middle class professional people, but can the same be said to be true of all cultures, classes and social groups?

Activity
You can find out more about Butler, Foucault and the postmodernists as well as what has come to be known as Queer Theory at *<http://www.leeds.ac.uk/ics/theory-r.htm>*.

MASCULINITIES

There is now a significant body of opinion that suggests that the focus on the study of gender must move beyond the study of femininity in an attempt to bring further understanding to the culture and behaviour of males. Increasingly there is grave concern that masculinity is a problem for society or that men have little understanding of what it means to be male now that their traditional dominance has been diminished. There are a number of American studies into the nature of changing masculinity and its impact upon the individual. Particular issues that support this type of position are exemplified by the following points:

- Suicide rates among young men are high and rising.
- There is considerable concern about perceived academic failure and under-achievement among boys.

DEFINING MASCULINITY

Kimbrell (1995) claims that there is a crisis for men and cites male unemployment and homelessness, anti-male custody laws and occupational pressures as leaving men stressed and vulnerable. He claims that they are pressured into a mystique of competitive and aggressive maleness that is media created and in which men will inevitably fail to measure up to the standards required of them. He supports the view of Pleck (1974) an earlier contributor to the debate who argued for a concept of masculinity that can accept emotional behaviour and challenge traditional stereotypes. However, the British feminist, Segal (1990) is less sympathetic in her claims that men are offered a variety of forms of masculinity. She argues for a new approach to gender politics and suggests that males will need to address issues of their own gender identity if they are to cope with the changing nature of female gender identity.

Certainly male identities have undergone some considerable change, and in the past were clearly class-bound. Segal (1990) suggests that Victorian middle-class males repressed their sexuality with cold baths, whereas working-class males expressed themselves through the ability to do a hard day's manual labour. As the twentieth century wore on, males were offered gender roles by the media, such as the cowboy or the gentleman, with which to identify. Brittan (1989) suggests that there is a difference between masculinity and masculinism.

- **Masculinity** is socially constructed and changes through history. It has been associated with care for the weak and with paternalism, but equally the new man offered a new masculinity in the 1980s.
- **Masculinism** is apparent throughout society and takes the form of a desire to dominate and control a social relationship or situation.

The future of men depends fundamentally on their own and the wider society's willingness to learn from the ways in which masculinity has been defined and constructed, used and misused in the past: a brave and imaginative appraisal will help make men's futures brighter and those of women and children too; a sullen, defensive refusal to do so may gratify some men but consign others to a bleak underfulfilment and much worse. The positive approach is essential: the modern world is changing fast and in ways which are rendering some of the old models of masculinity marginal if not redundant.

Hill (1997:2)

THE NEW MAN

The New Man was a seventies concept; feminists at the time claimed that sightings of the New Man were exaggerated. The New Man was seen as someone who would be a more caring, emotional and domestic person. Changes in employment practice and female roles certainly saw more men being willing to be seen to help in the home and to take on domestic responsibility. Belief in the development of the vulnerable New Man led to significant changes in certain areas of life, so that for instance, males were expected to be present at the births of their children. Young and Willmott (1973) found some evidence that men were helping in the home, but this has been challenged by Oakley (1981), who argued that their flawed methodology indicated nothing more than a passing involvement by men in household activities.

THE 'NEW' LAD

There has been increasing interest in the cultural phenomenon of the 'new' lad who, it is argued represents a return to the traditional male stereotype of being sport, sex and alcohol obsessed. This type of behaviour can be seen as being represented in magazines such as *viz, FHM* and *Loaded* and typical of television programmes, such as *Men Behaving Badly* and *Game On*. Laddism expresses characteristics typical of traditional male working class culture, but it seems in many cases to be a middle class stance. Nixon (1996) and others see the rise of the 'New' Lad as a return to many of the masculinities of the past. Note that the desire to care and protect for the weak is no longer part of laddism although it was certainly part of the masculinities of the 1930s and before.

MEDIA CULTURE AND MASCULINITIES

Feminists, such as Campbell (1995), have argued persuasively that working class masculinity has changed to the point where it is becoming a negative and destructive phenomenon. Young males are encouraged to define themselves as 'other' from females. Hope (1997) argued, in her work on the educational attainment of secondary school boys, that boys become locked into a stance which is 'not female' leading them to reject anything they view as female behaviour. Female behaviours include caring for others, working in school and being socially cooperative. By rejecting these social characteristics, boys become school failures and unemployable in the new service sector industries that require feminine skills. Females are willing to have their children, but not to marry or live with them also reject them as potential partners. Campbell (1995) points out that in the absence of a positive image of masculinity in the home, media images of masculinity become role models. Aggressive and violent films, such as *Goodfellas* and *Reservoir Dogs*, are viewed without their essential irony resulting in males being defined as masculine by their ability to exert power and control over others, rather than their ability to care for and to protect the weak.

Activity

Attempt a content analysis of any popular action film by noting acts of:

- Aggression by male characters
- Aggression by female characters
- Kindness or emotional behaviour by male characters

- Kindness or emotional behaviour by female characters.

What images of gendered behaviour are on offer for young children to identify with?

To develop this work, compare your findings with a dramatic film aimed at a female audience (a chick flick) or a cowboy film of the 1950s and 1960s. What differences emerge in the way that the genders are portrayed?

GENDER INEQUALITY

Despite the existence of the Equal Opportunities Commission and a variety of legislative changes which are supposed to bring about equality before the law, feminists argue that there has been less change in the status and position of women in society than many believe. They suggest that claims of female equality are exaggerated and further point out that only some females have benefited from shifts in society. Many women are expected to bear the double burden of work outside the home *and* domestic labour, which suggests that women may have lost ground in the fight for equal status with males.

- Employers have been successful in finding loopholes in the law by regrading certain jobs and segregating jobs so that it is acceptable to pay different rates (vertical and horizontal segregation). Over a period of years, women's average pay rates have been significantly lower than male average earnings and currently females earn approximately 70% of the rate for men. Caplow (1954) points out that many males justify low pay for women because they are seen as secondary earners despite the fact that many are primary carers as single parents.
- It is difficult to prove discrimination in any court of law, however, males and females are not treated equally in a whole series of spheres of life. Criminologists point out that women are more likely to be imprisoned on a first offence, while writers on social policy suggest that females take on the burden of care in the community.
- There is no measure of social attitudes that is really effective because most employers are expected to have an equal opportunities policy and pay lip service at least to the idea that males and females are equal. However, educational institutions such as schools and universities are notorious for

employing large numbers of women and promoting very few of them to positions of authority.

- Domestic roles influence career decisions. Women work in part time work and are paid less. They appear in the low paid professions that reflect their domestic concerns such as teaching and social work. Women's careers tend to have breaks due to maternity leave and equality will be difficult to achieve because women take on the burden of housework in many homes. Oakley (1974), in a survey of housework suggested that women spend an average of 77 hours a week on domestic duties.

GENDER AND CLASS

The association of class and gender has, until recently, been largely ignored by official sources. Women were not recognised as the potential 'head of household' until 1981, therefore all official statistics on class until this date assumed that men, as 'head of the household', were the dictators of the family's (woman's) class. Sociologists, such as Britten and Heath (1983), have argued that by ignoring the females' occupation in analyses of family class, official statistics may have totally misrepresented the class status of many households. For example, in a family where the woman has a higher-class status than the male, this may be the best indicator of the family's overall class status, because of the income differential and the access this provides to alternative life experiences and chances.

What is interesting about Britten and Heath's argument is that they accept female class **within** the confines of the family. In fact, most the analyses of gender and class within sociology have assumed a conjugal connection (see models below) and ignored the class status of single women. This would appear to be a massive oversight in a society where single status, for both men and women, is expanding as never before.

MODELS OF GENDER AND CLASS

- CONVENTIONAL MODEL – supported by Parkin (1972) and Goldthorpe (1988). This model supports the notion of traditional gender roles (man – breadwinner, woman – housewife), with the male's occupation dictating the family's class position and life chances.
- CROSS-CLASS MODEL – supported by Britten and Heath (1983). This model recognises that women are independent persons who in partnership may enhance the labour market and social class position of the family.
- CLASS ACCENTUATION MODEL – supported by Westergaard and Resler (1975). Partners originate from similar class backgrounds, which accentuates class inequality.

- PATRIARCHAL MODEL – supported by Walby (1990). Women should be seen as actual or potentially autonomous agents acting independently of men within the labour markets.
- INDIVIDUALISTIC MODEL – supported by Marshall (1988). Every individual in society should be assigned a class based on his or her occupation.

Activity
Postmodernist feminists identified that women experience very different levels of disadvantage. This has been supported by research into the social behaviour of middle-class and working-class women. Middle-class women may feel subordinated, possibly through lack of employment opportunities or progression, yet they may also employ working-class women as domestic labourers and therefore reinforce gender oppression within society. Conduct a survey to examine patterns of employment among women in your area. Are women employing women in traditional gender occupations? Are women employed in middle class occupations achieving advancement on the same level as men?

Summary and Conclusion

In this chapter we have looked at a number of elements of the gender debate and focussed on ways in which notions of gender are acquired and the impact that they have on the way in which individuals create their sense of identity and live their lives. Feminism has been a potent force for change in the ways that we perceive gender, but it is by no means a unified philosophy or social movement. Despite the work of feminists and of talented women of all kinds however, women as a group experience a number of forms of social inequality and there is some evidence to support their view that patriarchal society is basically misogynistic. Some feminists suggest that the concept of 'woman' is overplayed and feel that other social identities are equally significant to the life experiences of females. For example, black women experience racism and sexism, whereas working class women experience class based injustice and sexism. Postmodernists see gender as one of a number of possible social identities and suggest that increasingly, it is possible to create a personal sense of identity.

Individual males may support the aims of women, but there appears to have been some movement away from any progress that has improved the social position of women. Many people, including women, have rejected attempts to encourage women away from the domestic sphere. This may be seen as a reaction to feminism and the achievement of women in education and occupational areas where they have been allowed truly equal opportunities. Finally, given all of the social change, debate and movement in society, has anything changed for the vast majority of women? The evidence suggests not, the achievements of feminism may be confined to a few privileged people, whereas the vast majority of women are still relatively low paid, relatively low status and tied to domestic responsibilities which may give them emotional satisfaction, but which limit their activities in wider society.

Sociological Terminology exercise

Look at the following terms and be sure that you understand their meaning. Use them in your examination work:

Patriarchy; Feminine; Feminism; Masculine; Masculinism and masculinist; Black feminism; Sex; Gender; Sociobiology.

Group work

It is possible to identify gender stereotypes of gender by attempting a content analysis of any of the following cultural productions:

* Magazines
* Catalogues
* Clothing.

What impact does this form of socialisation have on the development of the gendered personality? Create a wall display of your conclusions.

Coursework

You could attempt to replicate the work of Pilcher (November 1993) and discover what women mean by feminism and how important the ideals of feminism have been in their lives. It works extremely well if you sample students. Ask women open ended questions about what they mean by and what they feel about feminism and then to give the same sample a closed questionnaire asking for a judgement on a number of positions which could broadly be described as feminist, such as equal pay or rights of employment. Interesting contrasts will then present themselves as women who claim to reject feminism will often identify strongly with certain aims of the movement.

The area of gender differentiation and social inequality forms part of all sociology so it is advisable to be certain that you understand the nature of the debate very well indeed. Males have dominated research for many years so that much early sociology disregards the experience of females, as well as of ethnic minorities and blacks.

Gender and its relationship to identity are such significant elements in all of the examination syllabi that you are advised to ensure that you fully appreciate the significance of this element of the course. An easy way to develop your understanding is to make it your own and to apply it to the real world so that it is not merely a set of theories in a book but a set of personal understandings. To do this, practise content analysis of the media so that you can find examples of ideologies implicit in production. Collect photograph and textbook examples of the ways in which males and females are differently represented and have different expectations made of them.

Develop an overview of how gender behaviour is learned and how patriarchy is maintained in our society as these are easy areas from which to draw questions for examination. The question of masculinity and male gendering is one that will continue to grow in significance in sociological debate. It offers some balance to the fury of the early feminists who were operating in a culture and a society which accepted male superiority as scientifically based in their different biology. Any answers that consider gender simply from the point of view of women will be self-penalising.

Evaluate the suggestion that gender is problematical for females in our society.
Evaluate the suggestion that gender is a form of caste in contemporary society.
Assess the extent to which masculinity is a fluid concept in our society.

This is a question which requires extremely careful analysis. Masculinity must be defined, but the term 'fluid' suggests that masculinity is a concept which is both changing and which has no set of rules. These two elements of the term 'fluid' need to be assessed. Certainly there are strong arguments to show that the nature of masculinity is changing and that a variety of role models are available. You might wish to look at the way that social class can be an element of notions of maleness so that working-class males gain status from domestic application of power and middle-class males experience power and status from the workplace. You might even raise the issue of postmodern notions of gender as being a matter of choice, but you would have to consider the status differences implicit in the choice of male and female identity. However, you have been advised to see all gender questions as being about the relations between two genders, and this perspective offers you the chance to address the notion of masculinity from a feminist perspective. Looked at from a feminine point of view, our society still retains many elements of patriarchy, so that while masculinity may change, it is still a dominant power in the social structure. Masculinity may be a fluid concept for men, but it still constrains women in their choice of lifestyle and their social aspirations, so it remains a concrete barrier for them.

Additional reading

See *Boys Don't Cry* in an attempt to apply your understanding of gender roles and changing gender identities. The film is about a Nebraskan youth who is born a girl, Teena Brandon, but who feels more comfortable as a boy, Brandon Teena. Brandon successfully lives the life of a male, courting girls with great success, becoming known for his caring and sensitive nature, while also having many male friends. However, one day his male friends discover the sex he was born and feel that they have been deceived and laughed at for their association with 'him'. Consequently they murder Brandon in what may be assumed to be an attempt to re-establish their own masculinity.

7

THE SOCIAL CONSTRUCTION OF AGE

THIS CHAPTER IS concerned with considering how age can affect the power, status and wealth a person enjoys in society. Each of the age groups considered in detail gives rise to a different set of social and moral concerns linked with the social construction attached to that age. The debates that emerge are ones of legal and social discrimination against children, which is based on a series of social constructs about the nature of childhood. Sociological discussion of adolescence is far more concerned with the origin and development of youth cultures. Many sociologists argue that they are in response to the marginalisation of young people in our society.

Although 'adult life' is barely covered as a topic in textbooks, this is not a measure of lack of interest. It is rather that adulthood is taken as the normal state of being by mainstream sociologists, which means that the study of all other age groups falls into specialist analysis. There has, however, been a recent development in late adulthood where many people are wealthy, fit and retired. These people are known as third agers, which adds a new area of interest to discussions of the elderly. Issues of concern to sociologists studying those of retirement age and beyond are the correction of negative stereotypes attached to the elderly and a direct concern with potentially discriminatory social policy.

Table 17: *Theories, concepts and issues in this chapter*		
WRITERS	CONCEPTS AND CONCERNS	KEY ISSUES
Turnbull (1972)	Social construction of age	Relative interpretations of age groups
Airies (1962) Newsons (1976) Oakley (1981)	Childhood	The social creation of childhood
Parsons (1954)	Functionalism	Youth and adolescence as a coping strategy
Clarke (1979)	Marxism	Youth culture – a return to working-class traditions?
Cohen (1972)	Interactionism	Media creation of folk devils in youth cultures
McRobbie (1991)	Feminism	Do female youth cultures centre on gossip?
Morris (1968)	Gerontocracy	The developments of age-sets
Townsend (1957) Outram (1989)	Old age	The effects of retirement
Lehr (1983) Goodman et al (1997)	Old age	Do the elderly constitute an underclass?

THE SOCIAL CONSTRUCTION OF AGE

The attributes that people place on words such as old or young are culturally and socially variable. Many cultures view old age as desirable; this is a time when people have earned respect and are viewed as particularly valuable members of society. Other cultures do not acknowledge childhood as being a separate state, so that children are expected to play a full part in the economic structure of society. Even within our own society, age forms part of a discourse so that adolescence is a recent concept which had little meaning for those pre-war generations who began productive work at the age of 13 or 14.

Activity

Ask a variety of people around you what three (or more) words spring to mind when they think of old age or of youth? You could always substitute the words 'grandparents' or 'teenagers'. An analysis of your results should provide you with the material to construct a social model of the way that people view youth and age.

- Count the number of positive associations for each age.
- Count the number of negative responses.
- Which responses are repeated most frequently?
- Do different generations, genders and ethnicities have different social constructs attached to concepts of age and of youth?

Anthropological writing has offered sociologists an insight into the cultural variations associated with age and the ageing process. Mead (1928) for instance, wrote about the arrival of puberty, particularly among young women, in *Coming of Age in Samoa*. Even though her book has been subject to later controversy with some of her respondents claiming to have lied, this remains a classic account. Turnbull (1972) wrote a devastating account of the Ik in *The Mountain People*. His accounts of the adults' attitudes towards their children are, by our social standards and treatment of children, some of the most distressing in print. The fact that children are cast out of their homes as young as three and left to fend for themselves, reflects the dislocation of the Ik and the loss of their culture after government relocation programmes designed to protect endangered African wildlife.

Biological evidence shows that all people experience physical change throughout their lives. That fact is inevitable. The evidence to suggest that different cultures view biological changes brought on through age in radically different ways is overwhelming and incontrovertible. Age is therefore a social construct and it is that concept which forms the theme of this chapter.

CHILDHOOD

The first, and best-known historical study of childhood was by Aries (1962). He argued that childhood is a modern social construction and that past ages viewed the experience of childhood as merely a form of miniature adulthood. He refers to norms about sexual behaviour and concepts of sexual innocence, which are very important in our culture and offers strong evidence to suggest that these simply did not exist. Interestingly, little has been written specifically on the social experience of childhood as such since the Aries text, though an enormous amount can be found in psychology texts and education texts concentrating on the social and mental development of children.

Activity

Collect a variety of images of childhood from the mass media; magazines will offer the best examles of photographs. Construct a wall display or poster to illustrate the social construction that we have of childhood. How 'real' or how romanticised is this view in your opinion? How differently are the genders represented? To develop the work, you could construct a male and a female set of pictures showing toys and other elements of socialisation.

Generally it is agreed that:

- The experience of childhood is typified by considerable inconsistency of practice and theory. Victorians had a rosy view of middle class childhood innocence, but were able to tolerate the employment of very young working class children. Child prostitution was not unusual and the Victorian public school was a notoriously bullying and brutal place. Equally, within our own culture, while many parents agree that video and television is a 'bad thing' few homes are without them and many children are allowed to watch extreme violence on videotape.
- The nature of childhood varies, so that in Victorian times, middle class children were tightly controlled and forced into very rigid forms of behaviour. In upper-class households, they would be washed and dressed to visit their parents for an hour or so a day, and their most significant adults were servants. Our own culture cossets children so that few are expected to walk to school and there are considerable constraints on their freedom of movement.
- Different cultures have very different views on parenting styles and the social and emotional well being of children. To illustrate the point, eight European countries ban the physical punishment of children whereas in Britain, the right of parents to hit their children is relatively highly valued.

There are cultural variations in child rearing practice so that you should note the following points:

- Gender socialisation is different for girls and boys. There are a variety of feminist accounts. Most notably, see the work of Sharpe (1976) and Oakley (1981) for considerations of this.
- There are social class variations in child rearing practice. Much of the work in this area was conducted in a series of surveys of children and their parents in Nottingham conducted by Newson (1976). The Newsons identified

authoritarian patterns as typical of working-class homes, and child-centred and liberal practices as typical of middle-class homes. As a point of evaluation, the Newsons relied on self-reporting of parenting styles. What people do and what they say they do may bear little relationship to each other.

- Parent/child interaction is variable, being influenced by class, ethnicity and the child's gender. Oakley (1981) identified a number of processes that are apparent in socialisation, and although she applied these notions to gender, they are applicable to all elements of the way in which parents and children interact:

  1 **Manipulation** – parents can encourage or discourage ways of behaving in their children on the basis of social norms.
  2 **Canalization** – parents will direct their children's interests towards appropriate activities.
  3 **Verbal appellations** – nicknames and chat often offer a child a clue as to what is expected in terms of behaviour from his/her parents.
  4 **Different activities** – parental activities with children will vary so that fathers will play football with sons and mothers cook with daughters.

- Ethnic minority groups (acknowledging differentiation among them) are likely to have a particularly high regard for obedience and respect in their children. Ethnic minority populations also tend to be younger than the whole population, but over the generations, they tend to take on the values and practices of the host population.

Activity
Contact Childline, the charity for offering support to troubled children, for information about their activities. You should not use the Helpline itself, but leave this free for those who require counselling. Send a letter or contact them through their website address at <*http://www.netexp.net/~mldunne/orgs/childlne.htm*>. Type Childline into any search engine and you should get results.

ABUSE OF CHILDREN

Note that childhood, whatever the social construct, is a very dangerous time of life. The danger is not usually from strangers, despite commonly held myths. Children are vulnerable to a variety of forms of abuse: by their parents, by adults they know, by other children and by the institutions of society. Most agencies recognise three types of abuse: emotional neglect, physical violence and sexual exploitation. Often though, all three types can occur within one family situation. One of the most serious problems with abuse is that it can be very difficult to define; so that often a measure of whether abuse has taken place or not is the reaction or impact of it on the victim. Few people are willing to estimate the extent and nature of child abuse, but you should note that a significant number of the murders recorded in Britain are of family members, particularly children by their parents or carers.

Study point

To illustrate the difficulty of defining abuse, consider at what point does hitting or smacking a child become abusive behaviour? Where would your group draw the line between behaviour that is acceptable and behaviour which should be illegal and punished?

YOUTH AND ADOLESCENCE

There are a variety of studies of youth and adolescence. Criminal and educational sociologists who focus on crime and education tend to examine issues of youth culture in relation to criminal activity or educational attainment. Within schools note that studies tend to concentrate on:

- the formation of youth cultures
- the influence of schools on future life courses.

Criminologists are caught in a series of debates associated with the question of why criminal activity and anti-social crime statistics tend to be composed of young people, particularly males.

Legally and socially, young people are subject to an inconsistent legal status and are marginalised from power or access to wealth. This is a very significant point in the following debate from the point of view of stratification and differentiation; do youth cultures originate in the marginalisation of the young adult from the mainstream activities of adult life? The following activity should illustrate the case to which young people are subject to an almost arbitrary system of legal and social controls which vary slightly according to gender and to sexual orientation.

Activity

List the ages at which the following activities become legally possible:

- Participating in a sexual act if heterosexual (male)
- Participating in a sexual act if heterosexual (female)
- Marry without parental consent
- Marry with parental consent
- Adopt a child
- Participating in sex education lessons in school if one's parents disagree with sex education
- Watching the sex act on a video or cinema screen
- Participating in a sexual act if homosexual
- Drinking alcohol without legal limit
- Driving a car.

Draw up a list of laws governing age that you find acceptable, and those which you find unacceptable. Do this as an individual, and then share this information with others in a group. Do patterns emerge?

Is THIS STYLE A SEPARATE CULTURE, OR MERELY A RESPONSE TO ADULT BEHAVIOURS?

FUNCTIONALIST ACCOUNTS OF YOUTH CULTURE

When looking at the variety of patterns of youth culture this century, functionalists tend to look at the purposes that these cultures have for society and to see them in a positive light. Functionalists such as Eisenstadt (1950) tend to see adolescence as a transitional phase through which people pass and which in other cultures is marked by a single rite of passage. He claimed that some individuals find this phase problematic and this gives rise to delinquency and deviance. However, Parsons (1954) offers us a view of the mass culture of the young as being related to the following elements:

- Changes in modern industrial culture which give rise to some increased affluence and wealth among young people
- Extended opportunities for education and college attendance which increases social dependency on the parents
- The effect of a mass media that allows young people an unprecedented access to cultural creations
- Parsons (1954) sees the function of youth culture for young people as a form of coping mechanism. Modern society is more individualistic than previous societies and so people can feel alienated; youth culture however, helps the adolescent to deal with a marginalised status.

Points of evaluation
- This view tends to ignore class patterns in youth culture. Hippies were a middle-class and intellectually inspired group of young people initially, whereas Rasta emerges from an Afro-Caribbean set of traditions and Punk was urban working class in its roots.
- Youth cultures tend to depend on peer group activity. Many youth cultures are actually exclusive of other individuals. Some individuals reject youth cultures. This does not fit the pattern of an individual phase through which young people may all pass. Thornton (1995), for instance, when looking at club culture suggested that knowledge of the culture was used to exclude those who did not have the knowledge and to gain status or 'cool' for those who did.
- Youth cultures are not necessarily benign and friendly to society. Many depend on aggressive drug-taking. Skinheads were notoriously violent and racist in many of their attitudes.

MARXIST ACCOUNTS OF YOUTH CULTURE

Marxists tend to view youth culture as evidence of a rejection of middle class values and proof of resistance to capitalist ideology. This stance is particularly associated with the Centre for Contemporary Cultural Studies among whom Willis (1977), Hebdige (1979) and Hall (1978) are the most notable researchers. One of the most notable studies was by Clarke (1979) who suggested that skinhead culture represented an attempt to return to the ethics and traditions of working class culture that had been lost. The stance of the skinhead was aggressive; for Clarke it represented an act of working class resistance to authority. It offers the individual a sense of shared community through an exaggerated style, the support for local football teams and a sense of territory. Note that Clarke has a tendency to gloss over the racist and neo-Nazi tendency that was espoused by skinheads. Corrigan (1979) tends to take an interactional line, so that while he notes that working class youth cultures reject conformity to the norms of school and middle class society, he also argues that this is part of an attempt to control and construct their own alternative social realities.

There are problems with this perspective.

- Youth groups are often in conflict with each other rather than with society as a whole. Riots in the 1960s involving the Mods and the Rockers illustrate this point. Both youth cultures emerged from London working class youth, and their differences seemed to be associated with musical taste and points of style. This contradicts the idea that young people are rejecting middle class society.
- Youth cultures are commercialised so that popular music, rather than representing a rejection of capitalism is actually a route to the acquisition of wealth. Consider the case of John Lennon, a member of the Beatles, who returned his MBE in 1969 as a protest against Britain's involvement in the war in Nigeria and for the support shown to the US in relation to the Vietnam War. Despite challenging the foundations of British traditionalism with this act, he went on to become very wealthy and to be internationally revered as a song writing genius. Many of the hippy and student based youth cultures of the 1960s and 1970s originated among young people from extremely comfortable backgrounds.
- It can be difficult to discern any ideology among certain youth cultures. Some youth cultures, particularly those that are self-destructive and drug based may have an ideology, but equally, many appear to be hedonistic. Is it possible that young people are simply about having a thoroughly good time?

INTERACTIONIST ACCOUNTS OF YOUTH CULTURE

Interactionists are concerned with the social processes that lead to the formation of youth culture and so there is a concentration on the role of the mass media in creating deviance. Cohen in *Folk Devils and Moral Panics* (1972) developed a detailed argument which showed how press reporting of some youth fighting on a wet bank holiday weekend when little else had happened caused public attitudes to harden and glamorised the scuffles into something much more socially significant than they really were. The young people concerned developed a sense of self-image derived from media accounts of their activities and this resulted in the creation of a set of behaviour patterns that could be described as a youth culture.

Criticisms of this perspective could include the following points:

- Interactionists fail to take into account the nature and impact of social class on actors.
- The role of the mass media in creating social groupings may be overemphasised.
- The interactionist perspective suggests that youth cultures are relatively short-lived, however, the evidence is that for some individuals, the attitudes and behaviours harden into something more permanent so that many people now in their fifties are still shaped and influenced by the ideals and beliefs of the hippies.

FEMINIST ACCOUNTS OF YOUTH CULTURE

This is an area that many feminists themselves consider to be profoundly under-researched. Youth cultures are frequently seen as a masculine activity with girls being allowed to participate, sometimes in return for offering sexual favour. This is very much the view offered by Willis (1976) in his study of 'the lads'. Part of the reason for this is that females are traditionally seen as home centred and family based. Male cultures are associated with the public domain of clubs, sporting fixtures and pubs. McRobbie (1991) and Garber (1993) suggested that female youth culture takes place within the bedroom; girls share gossip, clothing, make-up and magazines. They also claimed that youth sub-cultures reflected the masculine cultures in which they originate so that females are relegated to a secondary and sexual role. As a modern example, consider the way in which modern American rap music refers to girls as 'ho's', a thinly disguised version of the word, 'whore' or 'prostitute'; or 'bitches', which has no disguise at all!

McRobbie, a member of the Centre for Contemporary Studies, surveyed 56 working-class adolescent females who attended the same school, youth club and lived on the same council estate. She noted that their culture was centred on a very limited life experience based on school and their estate. They were able to reject the ethos of the school by adopting sexualised behaviours.

Evaluation of the youth culture debate

There is a significant and as yet unanswered question as to whether youth culture as a separate and distinct pattern of values and behaviours from adult culture actually exists, or whether such cultures do exist and then disappear again. Certainly, the commercialisation and the products of youth culture may arise in the streets and be a form of genuine self-expression, but they soon become ephemeral parts of mainstream popular culture and some of these forms are extremely short-lived indeed.

Activity

Saussure is widely considered to be the originator of the study of semiotics or signs. Hebdige (1979) suggested that one could apply semiotics to the clothing styles of youth fashions to see the underlying messages that they carry. Young women wearing Dr Marten's could be seen as using their footwear to symbolise a rejection of traditional femininity. Take any or all of the more extreme fashion statements of youth groups this century to see what underlying messages could be read into the clothing styles. Do they represent a rejection of adult cultural values as Hebdige claimed they did?

ADULTHOOD AND MIDDLE AGE

The study of society itself is a study of adulthood and middle age because this is the time when people are economically active and politically significant. While books and research offer little specifically under the heading of adulthood for the student to look at, obviously, we do in fact have wide knowledge of this age group. Similarly, few books specifically refer to 'men' as a social category, but we do know a great deal about them!

One of the most interesting developments of recent age analysis has been the way in which the boundary of old age has been pushed back as health care has improved and the age of retirement or late redundancy has reduced the age at which people can reasonably expect to complete their working lives. This period between retirement and the onset of ill-health or dependent old age is known as the third age and it is a significant part of the economic structure with products, leisure activities and luxury goods being targeted at this market. In terms of differentiation, the question is one of whether all people have access to health, wealth and high income in late middle age, or whether this is specifically a middle class phenomenon.

Activity

Suggest a variety of goods and services that are marketed specifically at the third agers, people of fifty and above. You could start with holidays and leisure services; think of Saga holidays and cruises. Daytime television offers a variety of advertisements pitched for the late adult market sector.

You may wish to contrast the positive image of direct marketing for the late middle-aged person with the negative images of extreme old age and disability which are typical of television programmes.

GERONTOCRACY

The role of elderly people in the family and in society varies from culture to culture. While their status in industrial societies tends to be low, in pre-industrial societies and rural societies, the elderly are considered have high status. Common myth suggests that many Chinese are flattered if you overestimate their age because age is considered positive, linked as it is with suggestions of wisdom.

There are a number of possible reasons to explain this:

- Societies that practise ancestor worship will revere the elderly as they are those who are most likely to become ancestors in the near future.
- Fewer people live to such an age as will make them elderly, and they may even seem extremely old at an age that in western societies would barely make them eligible for pensions.

OLD AGE

The role of the elderly differs from culture to culture, and the age that is seen as the onset of old age can vary depending upon the health of the general population. In many societies, the care of the elderly and infirm has been the responsibility of the family so that parents would have as many children as they could in order that some would survive to care for them in old age. In British society, there has been a relative increase in the proportion of the elderly in the population due to a decline in both birth rates and death rates since the Second World War. Women tend to have a longer life expectancy than men. This may be linked to physiological factors, but social factors such as the fact that smoking was considered a sign of immorality or low social class in females before the Second World War may have had an impact. When old-age pensions were introduced, it was assumed that people would die soon after retirement. Life expectancy has increased dramatically and over 15% of the population qualifies for age related pensions.

Field (1992) points out that census figures for 1981 showed that only 5% of those over 65 lived in residential accommodation. Well over 50% of people aged 65 and over live with a partner as half of a couple alone, or as part of a larger household with family members, a lodger or dependent. The elderly are not even distributed through the country either. Champion (1996) points out that many areas have very high-density populations of the elderly: spa towns, south coast resorts and rural areas. He also notes that the areas with the highest proportion of jobs for the young have low-density populations of the old.

One of the first and best-known books to study the lives of the elderly was Townsend's *The Family Life of Old people* (1957), which formed part of the Bethnal Green series. Townsend discovered that old people were happiest when they remained healthy and socially active at the heart of families, with older women taking on a matriarchal status and supporting their daughters. Older men tended to live short lives after retirement and he suggested that this was related to social isolation and withdrawal from male social activities following the loss of occupation.

There have since followed a series of studies on the sociology of ageing and many of these can be found in social work libraries or in social policy sections of bookshops. The perception of age generally offered in texts is that, as with disability from which the elderly are disproportionately likely to suffer, while the processes of ageing can be an inconvenience for the individual, many of the problems attendant on age are socially created. Difficulties with vision are made worse by the poor signposting and monochrome colour schemes that are typical of British public buildings. The elderly are often negatively stereotyped as being 'helpless' and those who experience the ageing process may be encouraged to have a negative view of their situation (Field 1992). A number of commentators point out that the elderly should not be viewed as a category as such, they are just as heterogeneous as the rest of the population and so advanced age should not be the most significant factor in people's responses to the old. We should see the individual and not the social category and the stereotype.

Activity
The charity **Age Concern** is active in promoting an understanding of age and the interests of the elderly. Visit their website by entering Age Concern in any search engine. You may enjoy a visit from some of their workers if you issue an invitation. Contact your local representatives via listings in Yellow Pages.

MYTHS OF AGEING

Outram (1989) points out that there are a number of myths commonly associated with ageing which should be treated with care, if not rejected fully. He lists the following points:

- Decline in physical and mental health is not an inevitable part of the ageing process.
- Many people do not want to retire and do not enjoy retirement, particularly since they experience loss of income and status.

- Most older people are fully capable of taking care of their own needs and do not become dependent on others.
- Many older people are in fact still caring for their own much older relatives.
- Women suffer from poverty in old age because they are less likely to have independent pensionable income due to their low position in the labour market or the loss of a partner's income on divorce or separation.

THE ELDERLY ARE AN UNDERCLASS

Old age can be considered to be a progressive loss of status. Lehr (1983) pointed out the negative stereotyping attendant on age as being linked with a progressive loss of many of the elements that we consider significant in our society: partner, health and occupation. If one takes the definition of an underclass as being a group that is in a low social and economic position, then the elderly and infirm who are dependent on welfare benefits fit the pattern of the underclass in British society because they are no longer part of the labour market.

Goodman et al (1997) point out that the average income of pensioners is around 75% of that of non-pensioners, and that the proportion has remained relatively stable over the years since 1961. However, they also note that pensioners have lower spending commitments; many have completed mortgage repayments and therefore own their own homes outright. However, pensioners still form a large proportion of the very poor because so many are dependent on state benefit for their whole income. Many more are clustered just above official poverty line figures so that were the official poverty line to be redrawn higher, then the proportion of pensioners would increase dramatically.

Most provision of care is by families, especially women, although males also care. The Equal Opportunities Commission suggested in 1990 that two thirds of carers are female. Many carers rely on benefits to survive particularly if they support those individuals who require supervision for 24 hours each day. George (1992) suggested that 50% of carers were themselves receiving old age pensions and that 55% of carers experienced stress. It can be assumed that the problem will become more politically significant as more females work and the proportion of the population requiring care expands. Families are smaller than they once were, and so the burden of care may well fall on one child for two elderly or demented parents over long periods of years.

RELATING THE DATA TO THE THEORY

- Marxists would argue that the low status of the elderly is part of capitalist ideology that punishes the non-productive.
- Functionalists would tend to view the debate as one which views medical advances as merely prolonging an inevitable decline and so question the value

of medical intervention. Field (1992) points out that this is a significant debate in the USA where personal medical liability is the norm.

- Feminists would see the withdrawal of government support for the elderly throughout the 1980s and 1990s as imposing burdens on families to look after elderly relatives with little in the way of community support.
- Interactionists tend to view the physical decline of the elderly as part of a negative image creation. They suggest that the loss of skills and self-esteem among the elderly is a response to social forces that devalue their contribution to our society.

Summary and Conclusion – the Association between Age, class, ethnicity and gender

In any discussion of stratification and differentiation, one of the main problems for theorists is that it is impossible to tell which of a number of variables are the most influential in reducing a person's life chances or influencing pay and conditions at work. It is during childhood that the patterns of socialisation that lead to adult behaviours are set in place. There are considerable variations between the ways in which children are socialised according to gender, class or ethnicity.

Gender socialisation of children offers the most dramatic examples of difference, but the other variables may arguably be more significant in setting up life opportunities and life courses. When talking of schools, Deem referred to an **aggregate of inequality**, claiming that all girls experienced discrimination because of gender. This discrimination was more pronounced for working class girls and ethnic minority girls who not only experienced gender discrimination but also race and class differentials too.

Discussion point

Suggest reasons why it would be so difficult to prove whether gender, ethnicity or social class is most significant in affecting life courses.

Age and social class are linked, so that the poorest among the pensionable population will also be those who were low or non-wage earners during their working lives. This tends to make women particularly vulnerable to poverty. State pensions provide a very basic income and successive governments have done little to increase their real value. This is a social class and gender issue as well as an issue of age, because those who survive on state pensions are likely to be those who have not paid into an occupational scheme and the low paid. These people tend to be women, members of certain ethnic minorities, the sick and disabled and the working class. In addition, women currently have a longer life expectancy than men, although this might change as smoking becomes increasingly a female habit. Both the Conservative government of the 1980s and the Labour government of the 1990s have encouraged people to pay into private schemes to top up their pensions through tax incentives. The implication of this policy decision is that the most vulnerable members of our community are those who have the least ability to secure themselves a comfortable and secure old age.

In conclusion, this chapter has been concerned with considering how age may impact on social behaviour. The pattern that emerges is one in which age is a very considerable determinant of social difference, but that other factors are also part of the picture. The next chapter will be concerned with how ethnicity can influence status and life chance.

Sociological Terminology exercise

Look at the following terms and be sure that you understand their meaning. Use them in your examination work:

Adolescence; Child; The third age; Old age; Pensions; Carer.

Group work

Take a variety of magazines targeted at various markets. Work out the social group at whom the magazine is marketed – you can do this by looking at the price, the content and the choice of front cover.

- Make a list of the products advertised.
- What values and ideas are attached to the various products? Look at the copy (words) of the advertisement to see which themes recur in the language of the adverts and the articles
- What perception of the various ages to which we belong do advertisers have?
- Does the image of the magazine offer a realistic or a stereotyped view of the age group that form its market?

Coursework

Qualitative study into the views of middle aged and older people into their feelings about old age would need to be handled very carefully. A young person could be seen as being patronising; however, you may be interested to test the discrepancy between social attitudes towards ageing and the views that people hold of themselves. You might develop this work by looking at attitudes towards ageing held by the very young compared to those who are more nearly approaching retirement age. It might be of interest to discover what people fear most about the ageing process. Is it personal, such as fears of loss of attractiveness or is it economic, such as fears of poverty or the fear of dependence?

Revision hints

In questions of age, it is always tempting to consider age as being the same as 'old' and to talk of 'old people'. Remember that age is a form of social differentiation that is cross-generational and that different ages have a different series of concerns.

Exam hints

• Assess the contribution of different forms of social stratification to the growing divide between rich and poor in Britain.

When examination questions refer to areas of stratification, differentiation or social inequality, remember to introduce not only issues of gender, class and ethnicity, but also age, as a determinant of unequal access to power, wealth and prestige.

8

RACE AND ETHNICITY

THIS CHAPTER IS concerned with how various writers have attempted to define and to use notions of race and ethnicity. For many of us race and ethnicity are terms which carry cultural expectations and on which we base value judgements about people's behaviours and contribution to society. The twentieth century has been haunted by racism, but it is not a recent invention; nor have widespread attempts to curb and control racism prevented ethnic cleansing and intolerance of people from minority cultures and religions. Ethnicity and race exist in economic terms in modern Britain; membership of an ethnic minority or an ethnic majority can limit opportunities to a person's position in education and employment. Ethnicity is also a cultural definition in that some people are labelled with expectations because they are visibly different, whereas others assume a personal sense of ethnic identity in order to reject people from cultures, which are different from their own. Recent theories, have suggested that forms of differentiation based on ethnicity may be more significant than class in offering us an analysis of inequalities in our society. In this chapter it is necessary to define race and ethnicity and to look at significant sociological debates that underpin a whole range of understandings about the meaning that ethnicity can have for people in our culture and the impact of that ethnicity on life chances.

Table 18: *Theories, concepts and issues in this chapter*		
WRITERS	CONCEPTS AND CONCERNS	KEY ISSUES
Myrdal (1944)	The existence of a race problem	Who defines race?
Swann Report (1985) MacPherson Report (1999)	The existence of racial inequality	Failure to recognise and act on racial diversity will create social problems

Patterson (1967)	Racial inequality is functional for society	What role do ethnic minorities fulfil for society?
Cox (1970) Miles (1982, 1993)	Uses Marxism to point out that ethnicity and inequality are linked	Racism prevents development of class consciousness
Hall (1980)	How do the media treat issues of race?	Race issues are a deliberate way of causing social dissension in a bid to draw attention from economic problems
Rex (1988)	Race and the development of the underclass	Race is a status issue and the working class see ethnic minorities as a threat to their livelihood
Modood (1991, 1992)	Ethnicity as a cultural variant	Ethnicity is a form of cultural identity to which people can aspire or which they can reject.
Small (1994)	Immigration	Black communities have formed part of British heritage since Roman times
Peach (1975)	Geographical location	West Indians and other minority groups experience the worst housing conditions
Brown (1982)	Work	Members of ethnic minorities experience disadvantage in the work place
Pilkington (1988)	Underclass thesis	There is little evidence to support this

THE SOCIAL CONSTRUCTION OF RACE AND ETHNICITY

The concept of race has been used as a classification system for people, by grouping them together through a common origin, since the sixteenth century (Cashmore, 1996). The physical differences associated with 'common origin', such as skin or hair colour, are known as phenotypes and presented an easy way to construct an identity for a 'different' group. Based on the work of Georges

Cuvier, a French anatomist, race became, and still exists as, a way of putting human beings into groups based on assumed differences in physical and mental attributes (scientific racism).

Morton (1839) described five main races: these are the Mongoloid human types, Caucasian, Malay, American and Ethiopian. Early anthropologists attempted to classify human groups into each of these racial types but discovered that the differences amounted to little more than the variety and distribution of body hair, body fat and some very minor skeletal variation in the development of long bones. Skin colour can vary from very pale to very dark in all of the racial sub-groups.

Much of this work has been superseded totally by genetic research, which has applied the idea that different races have different genotypes. The genetic make-up of the Ketchwa Indians in Peru allows them to survive better at high altitude. However, some sociologists, such as Herrnstein and Murray (1994), have applied the concept of genotypes to cultural and social characteristics, suggesting that one race is biologically inferior/superior to another.

All attempts to classify human types by physical and genetic characteristics are recognised to have very little scientific validity (O'Donnell, 1991). Indeed, it is now commonly believed by geneticists that all modern humans descended from a very few thousand original individuals. The concept of race may be an old one, but it is based on a series of misunderstandings about the nature of the human species. All humans are very alike genetically, with physical differences being no more than a reflection of a geographical/environmental origin.

It should be noted that although racial categories have no scientific justification, the concept of race remains very much engrained in our society. Consequently the significance of racial labels is great, functioning as tools to differentiate groups of people for whatever purpose is deemed appropriate at a particular time and in a particular place. Examples of 'the race tool' in action are slavery, apartheid and racial discrimination in the workplace. As Cashmore (1996: 298) states:

Societies that recognise social races are invariably racist societies, in the sense that people, especially members of the dominant racial group, believe that physical phenotype is linked with intellectual, moral and behavioural characteristics. Race and racism thus go hand in hand.

Ethnicity is interesting to sociologists, because it refers to a group of people who have a common origin and consciously recognised shared interests and experiences that make them distinct. We all belong to ethnic groups, but the strongest sense of ethnicity belongs to groups who experience disadvantage, such as immigrants or minorities. We define our ethnicity by a whole range of characteristics such as the language that we speak, the food we eat, our norms and values, the clothes that we wear and the beliefs that we share.

Ethnic groups tend to be referred to in a positive light, whereas racial groups experience negative associations resulting in racism. It is interesting to note that what we term as racism is a misnomer because there is far more variation, based on notions of ethnicity, between individuals in each of the racial groups than there is between the groups themselves. Racism is therefore an irrational intolerance of other people actually based on ethnic variation and cultural ideologies. Ethnic differences tend to be about culture and not colour. There are very few recognisable differences between Irish Catholics and Irish Protestants, but they were able to kill each other over cultural and religious differences in the past.

Activity

Elements of culture, and therefore ethnicity, consist of the following: norms, morals, values, ideology, food custom, festivals, religion and faith, language, music, laws, lifestyles, clothing, sporting custom, art, literature, leisure activities, choice of media, behaviour.

Decide on your own ethnicity and think of examples of each of the above which are particular to your ethnic group.

MYRDAL, *THE AMERICAN DILEMMA* (1944).

Myrdal, a Swede, was invited to the USA to consider the plight of the American Blacks between 1938 and 1942. Many lived in conditions of poverty, ill-health and ignorance and the government wanted an insight into this state of affairs. Courageously, Myrdal pointed out that the 'black problem' in the USA was in fact a white problem. Whites defined blackness, they created and maintained slavery and they assumed and enforced a sense of racial superiority. Because it is whites who assign the blacks their position, so the 'black' way of life is a response to the inability of whites to cope with blackness and black people.

Myrdal's concept of racism can be applied to the situation of **all** disadvantaged minority groups in the world, not only black ones. Ethnic minorities are subject to discrimination, and even violence, as a consequence of the majorities' inferior, socially constructed, definition of them. For example, half the world's states have recently experienced inter-ethnic conflict, with the attempted genocide in Rwanda of the Tutsis resulting in an estimated 250,000 deaths, while in Yugoslavia more than 130,000 people have been killed since 1991 (UNDP Human Development Report, 1994).

The notion of discrimination and prejudice has been identified in relation to race and ethnicity. At this stage in the text, it is also necessary to consider the difference between **prejudice** and **discrimination**.

- Prejudice implies a judgement made in advance. It is a mental perspective. The active term to describe prejudice is **racism**.
- Discrimination is what that prejudice becomes when it is translated into an action which makes someone less equal than others on the basis of a prejudice. Discrimination implies action. The term used to describe discriminatory behaviour is **racialism**.

Racial Discrimination. Also known as racialism this is the active or behavioural expression of racism and is aimed at denying members of certain groups equal access to scarce and valued resources. It goes beyond thinking unfavourably about groups or holding negative beliefs about them: it involves putting them into action.

Cashmore (1996:305)

Study point

To understand the difference between prejudice and discrimination, consider the phenomenon of the Irish joke. Collect as many examples as you can from the class. What is the nature of the Irish according to the jokes told? If someone were to believe the stereotype of the Irish based on the jokes, that would be prejudice.

However, the Irish are not visibly different from the majority of the British population and many of those of second-generation Irish descent do not even have Irish accents. If a person were to treat known Irish people in a negative way and differently from the rest of the population, then that would be discrimination.

RACISM/RACIALISM AND ITS CAUSES

Racism/racialism can be **overt,** such as under apartheid in South Africa where the government actively and openly treated black people as inferior to whites; or **covert** and hidden, such as in attitudes towards ethnic minorities in the workplace that are never voiced. It can be subjective, or it can be **institutional** in that the way that society works prevents certain ethnic groups from having the same opportunities as others. For instance, our society is Christian, and so Christian holidays are automatically offered to people. However, if religious days fall at other times of the year as they do for Jews and Moslems, people may be forced to take holiday leave for their own cultural observance.

Racial prejudice is ... 'An avertive or hostile attitude towards a person who belongs to a group, simply because he belongs to that group, and is therefore presumed to have the objectionable characteristics ascribed to the group'

Allport (1954) *The Nature of Prejudice*

INSTITUTIONAL RACISM
THE MACPHERSON REPORT, 1999

Stephen Lawrence, a young black A Level student, was murdered by a gang of white youths in 1993. He had been waiting at a bus stop with a friend when the youths attacked him without provocation. The police did not investigate the murder properly and the murderers did not get arrested.

The parents of Stephen Lawrence demanded justice through an inquiry. Six years later the MacPherson Report identified that institutional racism existed within the Metropolitan Police Force and that this was the cause of the poor treatment in relation to Stephen Lawrence's murder inquiry. It identified poor relations between the police and ethnic groups which should be improved through improved racism awareness training for officers. Sir Paul Condon, the Commissioner of the Metropolitan Police, acknowledged with a 'sense of shame' that institutional racism existed within his force, but that it was unintentional, rather than conscious in its application.

People may be racist/racialist and object to other people from different ethnic groups for a number of reasons. Explanations offered have included:

- **Fear of the unknown.** People are sometimes scared of people who are different and have different ideas and behaviour from their own. This fear can be cultural in origin, such as in Britain in the nineteenth century the Devil was commonly assumed to have black skin, resulting in black being associated with badness. Also, in rural areas where a high percentage of the population are white, ethnic groups are represented by the media, which may create a false and frightening image that cannot be challenged, because of the absence of social contact with that group.
- **Misunderstanding.** People may not understand ideas from different cultures. For example, in British culture, people look at you to show they trust you. In Asian cultures, it is rude to look someone in the eyes.
- **Stereotyping.** Some racial stereotypes are very threatening and people believe them without thinking. In the eighteenth century British slave traders developed and perpetuated negative stereotypes of black people, such as they were lazy, violent, untrustworthy, overtly sexual, to justify the appalling treatment they were inflicting on the black slaves. The Nazis were able to play on such stereotyping in their propaganda, famously comparing Jews to rats.
- **Ignorance and unintentional racism.** The Swann Report of 1985, which noted that failure of education to recognise cultural differences, identified unintentional racism within the education system and that the special needs attendant upon those differences were a form of racial discrimination. The MacPherson Report (1999) identified that unintentional/unconscious racism towards ethnic minorities existed within the Metropolitan Police Force.

- **Scapegoating.** People blame ethnic minorities for things that are wrong with their society. They claim they are taking their jobs or that they take the housing, even when these things are clearly untrue.

Activity

Attempt to make a list of all of the different forms that racism can take in a society. Consider education, work, leisure, and all spheres of public and private life.

You may wish to invite members of your local Committee for Racial Equality into school to talk to you. There are usually phone numbers in Yellow Pages under the heading 'Charities'.

THE FUNCTIONALIST VIEW OF RACE

In an argument that has been broadly discredited by later debate, functionalists such as Patterson (1967) and Banton (1983) tend to argue that it is functional for society to have ethnic minorities who are disregarded by the majority population:

- They can take on the worst occupations, that members of the dominant group do not want, based on need through social disadvantage.
- Their presence can provide an outlet for tensions arising within society as they take the blame for social ills.
- They will absorb the dominant social values of the host and be absorbed into society.
- They are a threat to scarce and cultural resources in attempting to realise their goals, therefore their position at the lower end of the stratification enables the dominant group to feel better in realising that they lack the talent and ability for high achievement in an equal opportunities society.

This form of thinking has been influential however, in that it has provided a theoretical basis for the political decision making of the **New Right** and their view that members of ethnic minorities must assimilate themselves into the values and cultures of their host nation.

Points of evaluation
- This offers the view that racism is somehow 'natural' and good for society.
- It assumes that ethnic minorities will wish or need to abandon their own cultures for the benefit of the whole society.
- It assumes that members of ethnic minorities will have equal access to the rewards of society and that they will not be marginalised into the worst jobs and will not experience disadvantage.

Suggest ways in which British culture has absorbed language, values and customs drawn from immigrant groups into our society. Start by identifying foreign words which occur in English. Look then at food, clothing styles, family structures, musical traditions, shopping customs and any other cultural accretions that you can think of.

MARXIST EXPLANATIONS OF RACE

People drawing on Marxism have added a great deal to the race and ethnicity debate. Cox (1970) and Miles (1982, 1993) both regard racism as a consequence of capitalism. They regard racism as inextricably linked with inequality and social ideology that sustain negative images of ethnic minorities through the superstructure, such as the media. Capitalists exploit working class racism to emphasise divisions within the working class and this hinders the development of class consciousness (Ben-Tovim and Gabriel, 1982). The existence of an ethnic *lumpenproletariat* provides a mechanism for capitalists to drive wages down, by ensuring that there is a cheap labour force that needs to be employed to survive. The racial stereotypes inherent within ideology are seen to justify the disadvantaged position of ethnic minorities within the workforce (Miles, 1993).

Hall (1980) in **Policing the Crisis** suggested that the racism of the British press in discussing the street crime of mugging acted as a screen behind which the government could hide a deepening economic and social crisis. However, there is a further debate within race analysis developed by neo-Marxists within the Centre for Contemporary Cultural Studies (CCCS), which is whether race should be considered as merely part of social class analysis or whether it has a significance that runs deeper. Neo-Marxists came to two conclusions, creating two models within the theoretical approach:

1 Relative autonomy model (Hall, 1980) – suggests racism is a historical phenomenon and works separately from social relations, but at the same time affects them. Consequently class and race should be examined together.
2 Autonomy model (Gabriel and Ben-Tovim, 1979) – racism is a product of contemporary and historical conflict, arising independently of class and social relations. Therefore racism cannot be reduced to class conflict, it exists as a consequence of ideological and political practices.

Solomos (1988) and Solomos and Back (1995) argue both of these Neo-Marxist approaches can be unified if racism is seen as part of the structure of each society, but with the realisation that each historic example should be studied separately.

Points of evaluation
- Marxism offers an excellent starting point for the study of issues of racism because it is a conflict model of analysis.
- Marxism offers an explanation for the exploitation of ethnic minorities, which is rooted in their position in the workplace.
- Not all members of ethnic minorities are poor and exploited victims of social inequality. There are some social groups who are in a position of some wealth and influence compared to their white neighbours. A disproportionate number of doctors, for instance, are Hindu and originate from the sub-continent.

WEBERIAN EXPLANATIONS OF RACE

Weberians such as Rex (1988) argue that race is socially constructed and is a form of ideology used to justify the discrimination that exists in society. There is a constant struggle for scarce resources and so ethnic minorities are targeted as a threat by the working classes. Rex (1988) examined race relations in South Africa and concluded that, based on class position and market situation, blacks experienced very real disadvantages compared to whites.

RACE AND THE UNDERCLASS THESIS

Rex and Tomlinson (1979) suggested that certain highly visible ethnic minority groups formed an underclass with expectations and life chances which were lower than those of the working class. Racial inequality affects black members of the working class because they have lower status within their class and are clearly visible as not being of the main culture. Members of ethnic minority groups are in a socially disadvantaged position because they threaten the livelihood and the wages of the working class due to their willingness to be exploited as cheap labour. The workings of racism conspire to keep black people in a socially disadvantaged position because they cannot then become socially mobile because of the rejection and racism of others.

It should be noted that Rex (1988) identified that the position of ethnic groups in the British stratification system had changed since the late 1970s. The rise of unemployment has undermined the position of the working class, pushing the white working class into a similar class position to that of ethnic minorities. The consequence of this, according to Rex, could be a unified class struggle of blacks and whites or increased conflict between whites and blacks in the increased struggle for scarce resources.

POINTS OF EVALUATION

- Marxists have been very critical of Weberians because they consider the Weberians to be over-concerned with status rather than class.
- This position offers some form of explanation for racism and the development of discrimination.
- The notion of the underclass has become a form of catch-all thesis to account for the disadvantage of a whole range of social groups at various times.
- Modood (1991) has pointed out that while members of certain ethnic minorities may indeed experience marginalisation, others such as African-Asians are not restricted to unskilled manual labour and have relatively high status occupations.
- There is no real evidence that the cultural values of members of ethnic minorities are completely at odds with the host society or that they form a separate social group rejected by and different from the white working classes.

POSTMODERNISM AND ETHNICITY

Postmodernism is a relatively new theoretical position in sociology that draws on the traditions of French philosophy. Much of its theorising is concerned with an interest in the notion of the 'self'. It considers that people have rejected old traditions of identity drawn from belief in fixed ideologies such as religion or Marxism and that many of us draw on a set of identities from which we can 'pick and mix'. The implications of this for the study of race and differentiation are dramatic and somewhat contradictory. Postmodernists argue that:

- People can draw on cultural traditions which are not their own and absorb them into their own personal identities. Culturally, race is therefore losing some significance and members of ethnic minorities should not be seen as 'victims' (Gilroy, 1987; Cohen, 1992).
- Some cultures are threatened by the possibilities of postmodern society and protect themselves by drawing on religious and cultural fundamentalism. This creates the possibility of resistance to a new global cultural form (Hall, 1992).
- Modood (1992) argues that ethnicity is a form of cultural identity to which people can aspire or reject, based on the distinct patterns of disadvantage that each ethnic group experiences.

Points of evaluation
- Postmodernism does not take account of the clearly described cultural and material disadvantage that members of many ethnic minorities experience.

- Postmodernism fails to account for the way in which ethnicity can be self-defining for many people and therefore underplays the significance of tradition among many ethnic minorities.
- Postmodernism does point to the variety of experience among different ethnic groups and suggests that to group members of various ethnic cultures together under the blanket term of 'black' misses the point that they are culturally very diverse (Modood, 1992).

ETHNIC MINORITIES WITHIN BRITAIN

We all have ethnicity; for many of us that ethnicity could be described as British. However, the British speak a language based on the interaction between a whole variety of ethnic groups which have become absorbed into the culture of the nation. These groups include Romans, Celts and the Vikings. Later waves of immigrants have seen the Dutch, the French and Germans all being absorbed into the culture of Britain. The Irish have been settling in Britain for hundreds of years and the black population have a long and venerable history as British, particularly in areas where sailors have settled. **Small** (1994) pointed out that many of the black people found in our towns and cities are descended from long established communities and the suggestion that they could be immigrants and therefore 'sent back home' is both racist and ignorant.

The term 'immigrant' though has become almost an abusive term among some groups of people. It is often taken to apply to groups of Commonwealth citizens who are not white skinned. This is a genuine injustice, because many of the non-white population who arrived in Britain after the Second World War had British passports, had fought for the British in the War and were encouraged to come here to undertake low paid, low skilled work or to fill gaps in the labour market, such as those in the health service. Once they arrived, they were subject to abuse and discrimination as there was little effective legislation in place to protect people from overt personal and institutional racism. Although many populations had settled in Britain through the 1930s the targets for racism and subsequent legislation often became those from visible groups who had different skin colour and were termed generically and inaccurately as Black.

Table 19: *Legislation affecting the rights of immigrants and ethnic minorities*		
LEGISLATION	TERMS OF LEGISLATION	PRACTICAL IMPLICATIONS OF LEGISLATION
1948 British nationality Act (Labour)	All Commonwealth citizens have the right to enter Britain to look for work and to settle	Many immigrants come to Britain to look for work or to excape political unrest in their home nations.

1962 Commonwealth Immigration Act (Conservative)	This restricted immigration	The terms of the bill applied to those from countries where the population is not white-skinned
1965 Race Relations Act (Labour)	Illegal to discriminate on the ground of colour, race or ethnic origin in providing goods, services or facilities	Beginning of equal opportunities for ethnic minorities in Britain
1968 Race Relations Act (Labour)	Race Relations Board given more power by the government	Community Relations Committee supports better 'race relations'
1969 Immigration Appeals Act (Labour)	The terms of this Act allowed those refused entry the right to appeal	Certain categories of family member were no longer allowed entry
1971 The Immigration Act (Conservative)	Commonwealth members are no longer allowed the right to settle in Britain	It became difficult for family members to gain access to Britain
1976 Race Relations Act (Labour)	Racialist acts, irrespective of intention, made illegal. Commission for Racial Equality established	Increased equal opportunities for ethnic ethnic minorities
1981 Nationality Act (Conservative)	This changed the terms under which people could claim citizenship of Britain	Immigrants had to be able support themselves and dependents financially on entry to Britain
1988 Immigration Act (Conservative)	This restricts entry to those with one British parent	Nationality became determined by racial identity
1993 The Asylum and Immigration and Appeals Act (Conservative)	Provided a right of appeal to asylum seekers, but restricted their housing rights	This further limits entry
1996 Asylum and Immigration Act (Conservative)	Only those with certain amounts of independent funding can enter the country	Further cuts in housing and social security entitlements

In practical terms, critics of government policy have argued that the impact of much of the legislation governing immigration into Britain has been racist. At the same time, there has also been equality legislation that makes overt racism illegal. Again, it is argued that much of this legislation has been relatively ineffective so that while overt racism is much more unusual than it once was, covert and institutional racism remains as powerful as ever. Reports, such as the Scarman Report (1981), have argued that members of certain ethnic minorities experience disadvantage in the workplace, education, housing and also when they experience dealings with the criminal justice system; which reiterates the need for more anti-discriminatory legislation.

It should not be forgotten that there are many different ethnic groups in Britain and that these groups have different social and economic experiences, reflecting the cultural diversity of a multicultural society. Some ethnic groups, such as Indians, have experienced great success with Britain, both in social and economic terms.

Study point

Out of 75 cases of black deaths in custody recorded here, only one has resulted in a prosecution (of the police) and only in one has the family of the deceased received compensation.

Institute for Race Relations website
http://www.homebeats.co.uk.htm

1 Suggest reasons why there have been so few prosecutions of the police for the deaths of black youths in custody.
2 Suggest how members of the black community might react to such statistical information.

ETHNIC DIVERSITY AND RACIAL DISADVANTAGE

There are practical problems in identifying ethnicity or race in our culture.

- Many of the categories ignore massive differences in culture and religion so that the term 'Asian' is used for a variety of peoples including Sikhs, Hindus, Moslems. Modood (1992) has objected to the use of the term 'black' to refer to non-white peoples because it obscures unique cultural developments.

- There are many who belong to more than one ethnic grouping as a result of cross cultural marriages.
- People may be unwilling to cooperate or distrustful of the motives of social surveys.

There was very little reliable data collected by government agencies before the 1980s and there has been much debate about the reasons for collecting such data since then. Gordon (1996) points out that

- The data could be used positively to respond to people and to aid them
- The data could be used with political purposes in mind and either create notions of victims or be used with racialist intent.

According to Anthias and Yuval-Davis (1993) the police use visual assessments based on skin colour and hair type. These categories do not take into account people's subjective experience of their own ethnicity and there is a degree of implicit racism in this process. The 1991 census referred to race (skin colour), ethnicity and nationality; this offered respondents the chance to define themselves for the purposes of research.

Despite the difficulties there is a massive amount of evidence to support the view that there are problems that face immigrants or people of certain ethnic minorities in Britain.

Language difficulties – until the 1976 Race Relations Act, many employers had rigorous language qualifications for even manual jobs as a way of excluding foreign labour. This was recognised by the Act and became criminalised. The children of immigrant families will experience fewer difficulties as they experience a British education system, but for older people especially females, language can still provide a barrier to social integration and take up of welfare services.

Cultural dissonance – Myrdal (1944) suggested that people who experience prejudice also experience despair.

Racial prejudice – figures produced by the *New Internationalist* suggest that Asians are fifty times more likely than whites to be the victims of racially motivated attack.

Poverty and poor housing conditions – people from ethnic minorities are four times more likely to be homeless in London than whites. **Peach** (1975) has shown that West Indians are most likely to be discovered in the inner city areas of poor quality and dense housing. Asian families were unable to rent and could not obtain council housing. As a result, they tended to buy the cheapest homes on the market.

Different educational patterns – both the Rampton Report (1981) and the Swann Report (1985) reported racial discrimination within schools and low achievement among some ethnic groupings. Many minority ethnic groupings are located in inner city areas where schools themselves are more likely to be described as 'failing' and which have relatively poor results. This in turn leads to poor skills or unrecognised qualifications which cause members of ethnic minority groups difficulty in high unemployment conditions.

Activity
Organise a class discussion to consider the following issue: are the difficulties which members of ethnic minorities experience in our society due to racism or their low status and class position in our society?

It is argued by Marxists that the poverty of the black underclass rests on racially discriminatory practices in the workplace and on the prejudice of working class people and organisations. Racism is not the cause of underclass status, but the underclass results from it.

THE UNDERCLASS DEBATE

- **Brown** (1982) pointed out that members of ethnic minorities tend to be over-represented in the lowest levels of the occupational structure. The average wage for members of ethnic minorities is below that of the general population. This is not proof in itself of either the existence of an underclass or that ethnic minorities form part of it.
- **Giddens** (1973) looked at the position of blacks and Hispanics in the USA in *The Class Structure of Advanced Societies.* He argued for the existence of a hostile underclass who would be forced to riot in the face of economic deprivation but who would not themselves become a force for revolutionary change in society.
- **Rex and Tomlinson** (1979) offer the suggestion of a dual labour market and thus support the underclass thesis. Non-Europeans work in the lesser labour market and are employed in jobs with few prospects or opportunities for advancement. They have fewer opportunities for training and so remain disadvantaged.
- **Castles and Kosacks (1973)** working within a Marxist framework reject the notion of underclass, seeing instead deep divisions operating within the working class which prevent the development of class consciousness. This reflects the work of Hall (1980) and *Policing the Crisis.*
- **Pilkington (1988)** rejects the underclass thesis because he argues that it is not supported by empirical evidence. A minority of males within each of the main ethnic groups is employed in work that is unskilled. He argues that members of ethnic minorities experience discrimination but that they are not so

disadvantaged that they actually constitute a group below the working class. He further claims that there are reductions in the extent to which members of ethnic minorities are located in the lowest skilled work.

- There has been a lot of American study on the issue of race and the underclass, possibly because of the clear ghettoisation of the Afro-American experience. Massey (1993) was favourably reviewed by Murray, and points out that nearly one-third of Afro-Americans live in areas where they do not experience contact with whites so that in practical terms, they are experiencing a form of apartheid. This segregation, Massey claims, results in poverty and alienation. Oliver and Shapiro (1997) however, see the problem as being one of gross inequality of wealth and power which is typical of American society. They argue that blacks do not have a poor work ethic or a culture which disinclines them to study or save. They suggest that racism and poverty create social problems for the blacks who form the underclass. The American debate takes place within the context of an agreement that an underclass of deprived black people does exist. While British non-white ethnic minority groups may not experience quite the same degree of ghettoisation as American blacks, many experience racism and poverty.

Conclusions

It is clear from the work of sociologists that while race itself is not biologically significant, it is socially significant in that racism is very much part of our culture. Ethnicity is a more sociologically useful concept, but it exists as a form of self-identification. While non-Asians may refer to people who may have originated in the sub-continent as Asian, it is a particularly vague term to use to describe the people who may have a wide variety of distinctive cultures, language and belief structures. Racism therefore is based on misunderstandings and misconceptions about people who are different from ourselves. Immigration to Britain is not a new phenomenal and people of different ethnicities have enriched our own culture in ways that we may not recognise.

Functionalists tend to consider that it is functional for society to have people of different ethnicity and they argue that people of ethnic minorities will abandon their own cultural values and become absorbed into British culture. Marxists however see racial inequality as linked to capitalism and social inequality. Racism is divisive of class and members of ethnic minorities are open to exploitation and poverty. Weberians offer the view that immigrants can and do change status and that racial inequality is related to times of crisis. When people are in competition for short resources they will find ethnic minorities a threat. More recent writers have considered members of ethnic minorities to form an underclass of poor and deprived people. Given that there is some argument as to the definition of an underclass, the position of ethnic minorities within that underclass remains open to debate.

STUDY GUIDE

Look at the following terms and be sure that you understand their meaning. Use them in your examination work:

Race; Racism; Racialism; Scapegoating; Ethnicity; Culture; Underclass thesis; Lumpenproletariat thesis.

Group work

Using the media, magazines and the Internet, create a wall display which offers positive images of members of ethnic minority groups. Try and avoid the stereotypes of sporting Afro-Caribbeans or black pop groups but aim for a balanced view.

Consider how easy or difficult it is to collect such data. What does that tell you about media representations of ethnic minority groups?

Coursework

1 Compare and contrast the attitudes of a group of white and non-white students to a particular issue such as success in education, or family. You will need a focus for this type of study, too wide a range of issues will make your study seem to lack structure.

Be cautious about approaching a group of people who are of different ethnicity from yourself and do not expect them to welcome your study simply because your intentions are good and you are a nice person. You will need to be fairly certain that you fully understand their cultural differences and that you do not patronise or insult through ignorance.

2 A study focussing entirely on secondary sources to establish that British society is unequal with regard to people from the different ethnic groups will be successful and presents fewer ethical dangers than a primary study. You will need to consider the debate about the usefulness and the reliability of official statistics with some care. You will need to address the issue of the underclass thesis in this study.

Revision hints

There are a number of areas to focus on with regard to ethnicity and to race and this particular topic offers examiners a choice of synoptic style questions that can draw on a number of themes surrounding the inequalities which some people experience in our society. You might like to consider, for instance, the issues of access to employment, education, legal services and representation, health and welfare and housing stock.

Remember that differences between ethnic groups are very significant and although the Irish have formed a large part of the immigrant community, they experience nothing like the amount of deprivation and poverty which are common to non-white ethnic groups.

Exam hints

With reference to any area of sociology which you have studied, evaluate the suggestion that despite the existence of anti-racist policy and legislation in society and in schools, there is still a significant amount of discrimination against members of certain ethnic groups.

You will need to show some evidence that you have an understanding of anti-racist policy and legislation with reference to your chosen study area. Sometimes this is codified in a set of laws, though in other cases there may exist a policy which in practice has no significance over the way that people actually behave with regard to members of non-white ethnic groups. You will need to prove discrimination too, but you should be wary of presenting all members of ethnic minorities as being the 'victims' of society – in many cases they are not, they are among the most successful and wealthy groups in our society.

Given the fact that we do have recent anti-racist policy, some groups remain disadvantaged and this is where your study of the underclass debate will be useful to you. You should also note that although government immigration laws are not racist in word, many have claimed that they are racist in intent because they act to disallow non-European immigration.

Additional reading

Visit the website of the Commission for Racial Equality at:
<http://www.cre.gov.uk/> . This is detailed and has some interesting links.

Those who actively oppose racism in any form would benefit from looking at the Institute for Race Relations website at *http://www.homebeats.co.uk/.htm* that is a valuable resource for those doing research into all forms of racism.

BIBLIOGRAPHY

Adonis A. and Pollard S. (1998) *A Class Act: The Myth of Britain's Classless Society* London: Penguin.

Aries, P. (1962) *Centuries of Childhood*, Jonathan Cape.

Barron, R. D. and Norris, G. M. (1976) 'Sexual divisions in the labour market' in Barker, D. L. and Allen, S. (eds.) Dependence and Exploitation in Work and Marriage, London: Longman.

Barry, N. (1999) *Welfare 2nd Ed.*, Buckingham: Open University Press.

Beechy, V. (1983) 'The sexual division of labour and the labour process: a critical assessment of Braverman' in Wood, S. (ed.) The Transformation of Work, London:Unwin Hyman.

Bottomore, T. B. (1966) *Elites and Society* Harmondsworth: Penguin.

Braham, P., Rattansi, A. and Skellington, R. (eds.) (1992) *Racism and Antiracism*, London: Sage.

Brittan, Arthur (1989) *Masculinity and Power*, Oxford: Blackwell.

Brown, M. and Madge, N. (1982) *Despite the Welfare State: A Report on the SSRC/DHSS Programme of Research into Transmitted Deprivation*, London: Heinemann

Bulmer and Solomos (1999) *Racism*, Oxford: Oxford University Press.

Butler, J. (1993) *Bodies that Matter*, London: Routledge.

Butler, J. (1999) *Gender Trouble (Tenth Anniversary Edition): Feminism and the Subversion of Identity*, London: Routledge,

Campbell, B. (1993) *Goliath: Britain's Dangerous Places*, London: Methuen.

Carrington, W.J, McCue, K. and Pierce, B. (1995) *The Role of Employer/Employee Interactions in Labor Market Cycles: Evidence from the Self-Employment.*

Clarke, J. (1979) *The Skinheads and the Study of Youth Culture* Birmingham: CCCS.

Cohen, S. (1972) *Folk Devils and Moral Panics*, London: Paladin.

Crewe, I. (1992) *'Why did Labour lose (yet again)?' Politics Review*, September.

Dahrendorf, R. (1959) Class and Class Conflict in an Industrial Society, London: Routledge and Kegan Paul.

Dahrendorf, R. (1992) *Understanding the Underclass*, London: Policy Studies Institute.

Davis, K. and Moore, W. E. (1967) *'Some principles of stratification'* in Bendix, R. and Lispet, S. M. *Class, Status and Power*, London: Routledge and Kegan Paul.

Edgell, S. (1993) *Class*, London: Routledge.

Engels, Frederick (1968) 'The origin of family, private property and state' in Marx, Karl and Engels, Frederick *Selected Works in One Volume*, London: Lawrence and Wishart

Faludi, S. (1992) *Backlash: The Undeclared War against Women*, London: Chatto and Windus.

Field, D. (1992) *'Elderly people in British society'* in *Sociology Review*, April 1992.

Firestone, S. (1970) *The Dialetic of Sex*, London: Women's Press.

Garber, M. (1993) *Vested Interests,* London: Penguin.

George, V. and Page, R. (1995) *Modern Thinkers on Welfare,* London: Prentice Hall.

Giddens, A. (1973) *The Class Structures of Advanced Societies,* London, Hutchinson.

Giddens, A. (1984) *The Constitution Society: An Outline of the Theory of Structuration,* Cambridge, Polity Press.

Gilroy, P. (1991) *There Ain't No Black in the Union Jack.* Harmondsworth: Penguin.

Goldthorpe, J. (1987) *Social Mobility and the Class Structure in Modern Britain,* Oxford, Clarendon Press.

Goldthorpe, J. H. (in collaboration with Catriona Llewellyn and Clive Payne) (1980) *Social Mobility and Class Structure in Modern Britain* Oxford: Clarendon Press

Goldthorpe, J. H.Lockwood, D. Bechofer, F. and Platt, J. (1968) *The Affluent Worker: Industrial Attitudes; The Affluent Worker, Political Attitudes and Behaviour* and *The Affluent Worker in the Class Structure,* Cambridge: Cambridge University Press.

Goodman, A. Johnson, P. and Webb, S. (1997) *Inequality in the UK* Oxford: OUP.

Gordon, D. (2000) 'Inequalities in income, wealth and standard of living in Britain' in Pantazis, C. and Gordon, D. (eds.) *Tackling Inequalities,* Bristol: The Policies Press.

Gordon, P. (1989) *Citizenship for Some? Race and Government Policy 1979–89,* London: Runnymede Trust.

Gouldner, A. (1975) *For Sociology,* Harmondsworth: Penguin.

Gramsci, A. (1971) *Selections From the Prison Notebooks,* London: Lawrence and Wishart.

Greer, G. (1970) *The Female Eunuch,* St Albans: Paladin.

Gregg, Paul (1994) 'Out of court again!: A social scientist's analysis of the unemployment statistics in the UK', in *Journal of the Royal Statistical Society Series A,* No 157.

Halsey, A. Heath, A. and Ridge, J. M. (1980) *Origins and Destinations,* Oxford: Clarendon Press.

Heath, A. (1981) *Social Mobility,* London, Fontana.

Hebdige, D. (1979) *Subculture: The Meaning of Style,* London: Methuen.

Hill, D. (1997) *The Future of Men,* London: Phoenix.

Hill Collins, P. (1990) *Black Feminist Thought: Knowledge, Consciousness, and the Politics of Empowerment,* Boston: Unwin Hyman.

HMSO (1992) Social Trends, London: HMSO.

Home Office (1981) *Racial Attacks,*London: HMSO.

Hope, T. (1997) 'A question of underachievement? Boys and secondary education' *Social Science Teacher,* Vol.26, No.3, Summer.

Hutton, W. (1995) *The State We're In,* London: Jonathon Cape.

Jones, T. (1993) *Britain's Ethnic Minorities,* London: PSI.

Keith, M. (1993) *Race, Riots and Policing,* London: UCL Press.

Kimbrell, Andrew, (1995) *Masculine Mystique: The Politics of Masculinity*, New York: Ballantyne.

Lehr, U. (1983) 'Stereotypes of ageing and age norms' in Birren, J. E. (ed) *Ageing: A Challenge to Science and Society*, Vol. 3, Oxford: Oxford University Press.

Lockwood, D. (1989) *The Blackcoated Worker: A Study in Class Consciousness* 2nd ed, Oxford: Clarendon.

Low Pay Commission (2000) *http://www.lowpay.gov.uk/* Manchester, Low Pay Unit.

Marsland, D (1989) 'Universal welfare provision creates dependant population' in *Social Studies Review*.

Marx, K. (1954) *Capital*, Vol. 1, London: Lawrence and Wishart (original publication 1867).

Marx, K. and Engels, F. (1998) *The Communist Manifesto*, London: Verso (original publication 1888).

McRobbie, A. (1991) *Feminism and Youth Culture: from 'Jackie' to 'Just Seventeen'*, Basingstoke: Macmillan Education.

Mead, L. (1985) *Beyond Entitlement*, New York: Basic Books.

Miliband, R. (1973) *The State of Capitalist Society: Analysis of the Western System of Power*, London: Quartet Books.

Millerson, G. (1964) *The Qualifying Professions*, New York, Free Press.

Millet, K. (1970) *Sexual Politics*, New York: Doubleday.

Mills, C. Wright (1964) *White Collar: The American Middle Classes*, New York: Oxford University Press.

Mirza, H, S. (1997) *Black British Feminism*, London, Routledge.

Morris, D. R/ (1968) *The Washing of the Spears*, London: Sphere Books.

Murray, C. (1984) *Losing Ground*, New York: Basic Books.

Murray, C. (1996) *Underclass: The Crisis Deepens*, London: The Institute of Economic Affairs.

Newson, J.and E. (1976) *Seven Years Old in the Home Environment*, London: Allen and Unwin.

Nixon, S. (1996) *Hard Looks*, UCL Press.

Oakley, A. (1974) *Housewife: The Sociology of Housework*, Oxford: Martin Robertson.

Oakley, A. (1981) *Subject Women*, Oxford: Martin Robertson.

Oakley, A. (1986) *From Here to Maternity: Becoming a Mother* Harmondsworth: Penguin.

Outram, S. (1989) *Sociology in Focus: Social Policy*, London: Longman.

Paglia, Camille (1994) *Vamps and Tramps: New Essays*, London: Viking.

Pahl, R. E. and Wallace, C. (1988) 'Neither angels in marble nor rebels in red' in Robson, D. Martin (1999) 'Self-employment in the UK regions' in *Applied Economics*, Volume 30, issue 3.

Parkin, F. (1979) *Marxism and Class Theory: A Bourgeois Critique*, London: Tavistock.

Parsons, T. (1951) *The Social System*, New York: Free Press.

Peach, Ceri (ed.) (1975) *Urban social segregation* London : Longman

Pilkington, A. (1999) 'The underclass revisited' *Social Science Teacher*, Vol 29, No. 1.

Pleck, Joseph (1974) *Men & Masculinity*, New York: Prentice Hall.

Ramos, X. (unpublished doctoral thesis) 'Earnings inequality and earnings mobility in Great Britain: evidence from the BHPS, 1991–94' Sosig website: Institute for Social and Economic Research, University of Essex.

Runciman, W. G. (1990) 'How many classes are there in contemporary British society?' *Sociology*, Volume 4, No, 3,

Saunders, P. (1990) *Social Class and Stratification*, London: Routledge.

Saunders, P. (1995) *Capitalism: A Social Audit*, Buckingham: Open University Press.

Savage, M. (1995) 'The Middle Classes in Modern Britain' in *Sociology Review*, November 1995.

Scott, J. (1982) *The Upper Classes*, London: Macmillan.

Scott, J. (1986) 'Does Britain still have a ruling class?' *Social Studies Review*, Volume 2 , No. 1.

Scruton, R. (1986) *Sexual Desire: A Philosophical Investigation*, London: Weidenfeld and Nicolson.

Segal, L. (1990) in *Slow Motion: Changing Masculinities, Changing Men* New York: Rutgers University Press.

Sharpe, Sue (1976*) Just like a Girl: How Girls Learn to be Women*, Harmondsworth: Penguin.

Simon, W. (1996) 'The postmodernization of sex and gender' in Anderson, W. T. (ed.) *The Fontana Post-Modernism Reader*, London: Fontana.

Skellington, R. and Morris, P. (1996) (2nd ed) *'Race' in Britain Today*, London: Sage.

Solomos, J. (1989) *Race and Racism in Contemporary Britain*. Basingstoke: Macmillan.

Thornton, Sarah (1995) *Club Cultures, Music Media and Subcultural Capital*, Cambridge: Polity Press.

Tinker, A. (1984) *The elderly in Modern Society*, (2nd ed.), London: Longman.

Townsend, P. (1957) *The Family Life of Old People: An Inquiry in East London*, London: Routledge and Kegan Paul.

Tumin, M. (1967) *Social Stratification: The Forms and Functions of Social Inequality*, New York: Prentice Hall.

Turak, I. (2000) 'Inequalities in employment' in Pantazis, C. Gordon, D. (eds.) (2000) *Tackling Inequalities*, Bristol: The Policies Press.

Turnbull, C. (1972) *The Mountain People*, New York: Simon and Schuster.

Walby, S. (1990) *Theorizing Patriarchy*, Oxford: Blackwell.

Weber, M. (1985) *The Protestant Ethic and the Spirit of Capitalism*, London, Unwin (original publication 1905).

Westergaard, J. and Resler, H. (1975) *Class in a Capitalist Society*, London: Penguin.

Wilkinson, R. (1996) 'Inequality kills', *Observer*, 8 September 1996.

Wright, E. O. (1997) *Class Counts*, Cambridge: Cambridge University Press.

Wright Mills, C. (1956) *White Collar*, Oxford: Oxford University Press.

INDEX